HOW TO

GEORGE TARGET
thirty years. His many
novels and non-fiction on a variety of topics, as well as
numerous articles for magazines and newspapers. He
has also appeared frequently on TV and radio. He is
married, and lives in Norfolk.

Overcoming Common Problems Series

The ABC of Eating
Coping with anorexia, bulimia and compulsive eating
JOY MELVILLE

An A–Z of Alternative Medicine
BRENT Q. HAFEN AND KATHRYN J. FRANDSEN

Arthritis
Is your suffering really necessary?
DR WILLIAM FOX

Being the Boss
STEPHEN FITZSIMON

Birth Over Thirty
SHEILA KITZINGER

Body Language
How to read others' thoughts by their gestures
ALLAN PEASE

Calm Down
How to cope with frustration and anger
DR PAUL HAUCK

Comfort for Depression
JANET HORWOOD

Common Childhood Illnesses
DR PATRICIA GILBERT

Complete Public Speaker
GILES BRANDRETH

Coping with Depression and Elation
DR PATRICK McKEON

Coping Successfully with Your Child's Asthma
DR PAUL CARSON

Coping Successfully with Your Child's Skin Problems
DR PAUL CARSON

Coping Successfully with Your Hyperactive Child
DR PAUL CARSON

Curing Arthritis Cookbook
MARGARET HILLS

Curing Arthritis – The Drug-free Way
MARGARET HILLS

Curing Illness – The Drug-free Way
MARGARET HILLS

Depression
DR PAUL HAUCK

Divorce and Separation
ANGELA WILLANS

The Epilepsy Handbook
SHELAGH McGOVERN

Everything You Need to Know about Adoption
MAGGIE JONES

Everything You Need to Know about Contact Lenses
DR ROBERT YOUNGSON

Everything You Need to Know about the Pill
WENDY COOPER AND TOM SMITH

Everything You Need to Know about Shingles
DR ROBERT YOUNGSON

Family First Aid and Emergency Handbook
DR ANDREW STANWAY

Feverfew
A traditional herbal remedy for migraine and arthritis
DR STEWART JOHNSON

Fight Your Phobia and Win
DAVID LEWIS

Flying Without Fear
TESSA DUCKWORTH AND DAVID MILLER

Goodbye Backache
DR DAVID IMRIE WITH COLLEEN DIMSON

Good Publicity Guide
REGINALD PEPLOW

Helping Children Cope with Grief
ROSEMARY WELLS

How to Be Your Own Best Friend
DR PAUL HAUCK

How to Control your Drinking
DRS W. MILLER AND R. MUNOZ

Overcoming Common Problems Series

How to Cope with Stress
DR PETER TYRER

How to Cope with your Child's Allergies
DR PAUL CARSON

How to Cope with your Nerves
DR TONY LAKE

How to Cope with Tinnitus and Hearing Loss
DR ROBERT YOUNGSON

How to Do What You Want to Do
DR PAUL HAUCK

How to Enjoy Your Old Age
DR B. F. SKINNER AND M. E. VAUGHAN

How to Interview and Be Interviewed
MICHELE BROWN AND GYLES BRANDRETH

How to Improve Your Confidence
DR KENNETH HAMBLY

How to Love a Difficult Man
NANCY GOOD

How to Love and be Loved
DR PAUL HAUCK

How to Make Successful Decisions
ALISON HARDINGHAM

How to Pass Your Driving Test
DONALD RIDLAND

How to Say No to Alcohol
KEITH McNEILL

How to Sleep Better
DR PETER TYRER

How to Stand up for Yourself
DR PAUL HAUCK

How to Start a Conversation and Make Friends
DON GABOR

How to Stop Feeling Guilty
DR VERNON COLEMAN

How to Stop Smoking
GEORGE TARGET

How to Stop Taking Tranquillisers
DR PETER TYRER

If Your Child is Diabetic
JOANNE ELLIOTT

Jealousy
DR PAUL HAUCK

Learning to Live with Multiple Sclerosis
DR ROBERT POVEY, ROBIN DOWIE AND GILLIAN PRETT

Living with Grief
DR TONY LAKE

Living Through Personal Crisis
ANN KAISER STEARNS

Living with High Blood Pressure
DR TOM SMITH

Loneliness
DR TONY LAKE

Making Marriage Work
DR PAUL HAUCK

Making the Most of Loving
GILL COX AND SHEILA DAINOW

Making the Most of Yourself
GILL COX AND SHEILA DAINOW

Making Relationships Work
CHRISTINE SANDFORD AND WYN BEARDSLEY

Meeting People is Fun
How to overcome shyness
DR PHYLLIS SHAW

Nervous Person's Companion
DR KENNETH HAMBLY

One Parent Families
DIANA DAVENPORT

Overcoming Fears and Phobias
DR TONY WHITEHEAD

Overcoming Stress
DR VERNON COLEMAN

Overcoming Tension
DR KENNETH HAMBLY

Overcoming Common Problems Series

The Parkinson's Disease Handbook
DR RICHARD GODWIN-AUSTEN

Second Wife, Second Best?
Managing your marriage as a second wife
GLYNNIS WALKER

Self-Help for your Arthritis
EDNA PEMBLE

Six Weeks to a Healthy Back
ALEXANDER MELLEBY

Sleep Like a Dream – The Drug-free Way
ROSEMARY NICOL

Solving your Personal Problems
PETER HONEY

Someone to Love
How to find romance in the personal columns
MARGARET NELSON

A Step-Parent's Handbook
KATE RAPHAEL

Stress and your Stomach
DR VERNON COLEMAN

Trying to Have a Baby?
Overcoming infertility and child loss
MAGGIE JONES

What Everyone Should Know about Drugs
KENNETH LEECH

Why Be Afraid?
How to overcome your fears
DR PAUL HAUCK

You and Your Varicose Veins
DR PATRICIA GILBERT

Your Arthritic Hip and You
GEORGE TARGET

Overcoming Common Problems

HOW TO STOP SMOKING

George Target

Illustrated by Andy Collis

SHELDON PRESS
LONDON

First published in Great Britain in 1986 by
Sheldon Press, SPCK, Marylebone Road, London NW1 4DU

Copyright © George Target 1986

Second impression 1988

All rights reserved. No part of this book may be reproduced or transmitted in any form or by any means, electronic or mechanical, including photocopying, recording or by any information storage or retrieval system, without permission in writing from the publisher.

Thanks are due to Frances Lincoln Ltd for permission to quote extracts from *Health and Fitness Handbook* by Miriam Stoppard. An extract has also been quoted from an article in *The Listener*, 1971, by Dr Henry Miller. Despite diligent enquiry, it has proved impossible to trace the copyright holder, and the author and publisher therefore extend their sincere apologies.

Thanks are also due to Andy Collis and the Stanborough Press Ltd for permission to reproduce the illustrations in this book.

British Library Cataloguing in Publication Data

Target, George
 How to stop smoking.——(Overcoming common problems)
 1. Cigarette habit
 I. Title II. Series
 613.8'5   HV5740

ISBN 0–85969–499–2
ISBN 0–85969–500–X Pbk

Typeset by Deltatype, Ellesmere Port
Printed in Great Britain by
Richard Clay Ltd, Bungay, Suffolk

Contents

	Introduction	1
1	Excuses, Excuses	5
2	What Sort of Smoker Are You?	13
3	Ways of Stopping	22
4	Using the Mind to Stop	39
5	Some of the Means of Stopping	45
6	Stopping on Your Own	62
7	Stopping With the Help of Somebody Else	95
8	Staying Stopped	100

Introduction

This book is about how to stop smoking.

It isn't a protest at smoking, it doesn't make intentionally hurtful remarks about the supposed stupidity and selfishness of smokers, it can't be bothered with jumping up and down in the pulpit over the commercial policies and activities of the tobacco companies, and it refuses to get excited at the successive governments which have derived such vast revenues from taxing what is the second most dangerous threat to the health and happiness of their citizens.

All it offers to do is show how you can stop smoking . . . if you want to.

That's the important bit: if you want to.

If you are not yet persuaded that there are at least some good reasons for stopping, then you'd waste your money to buy it, and your time in reading past this page.

The fact that you have got this far is an indication that you are interested in the possibility of stopping. You have made a choice — and stopping is about choosing.

All of your smoking life you've been choosing: you chose to start, you've chosen your favourite brand, until now you've chosen to go on smoking . . . and here you are considering the choice of stopping.

It doesn't yet matter what your reasons for stopping are: better health and less chance of dying before your time, improved appearance, increased self-confidence, greater sexiness, saving money, a more intense enjoyment of all the pleasures of life . . . only so long as you believe that you'd be happier and better off in one or more ways if you didn't smoke.

*   *   *

The book doesn't suggest that you should cut down your

smoking to a 'safe' or even 'safer' level, that you should change your brand to one with a lower tar content, that you should switch to cigars or a pipe, or to any of the various tobacco substitutes.

What it does say is that, if you want to stop smoking, you can: not smoulder on, but stop altogether while you're at it.

The only absolutely safe cigarette is an unlit one.

Because of all those people who smoke more than one cigarette during adolescence, seven out of ten will go on smoking for thirty or forty years. Only the teenager who has never tried to smoke, or who tried and didn't like it and had the courage to refuse to go on trying, has much chance of growing into a non-smoking and healthy adult.

One cigarette.

In fact, it's far easier to become dependent on cigarettes after that first one than it is to become dependent on alcohol. Most drinkers aren't alcoholics, but not more than two out of a hundred smokers succeed in remaining occasional smokers.

The stopping is easy

To stop is much easier than many smokers imagine.

True, most do believe that it's difficult, if not impossible — or hardly worth the misery. Some have tried to stop, and failed, and haven't got the heart to try again. And some will undoubtedly find it harder than others.

Merely stopping, and hoping that you'll stay stopped by will power, is to ask for that misery, invite failure, and end back where you started on forty or fifty a day.

To stop and stay stopped you have to *think* about stopping, prepare to stop, make it quite an occasion, follow a simple and pleasurable routine for a few days, take some rather obvious precautions against being tempted to start again . . . and then you're a non-smoker.

'If you want to give up smoking,' says Miriam Stoppard, 'there is nothing that can stop you.'

And she should know.

INTRODUCTION

She stopped.
And so have nine million other people in this country.
Now, it's *your* turn.

1
Excuses, Excuses

Most non-smokers accept that smoking is as dangerous as doctors state, but less than half the smokers don't think that it's as dangerous as all that: 'You know, bit exaggerated.'

And most smokers claim that they've got 'every moral right' to behave in ways which might injure them: 'Like seat-belts — what's it got to do with anybody else?'

Have they ever thought about the doctors and nurses who will be obliged to care for them when the heart and lungs are affected?

'Well, they get paid for doing it, don't they?'

But, despite all the excuses and evasions and wry jokes, smokers know about the grave dangers to health and life caused by smoking.

Many, perhaps six or seven out of ten, would like to stop, but have tried and failed — or haven't yet tried.

And most of these would-be stoppers probably feel guilty about either not stopping or not being able to. Every new statistic on the incidence of lung cancer is a reminder of their own failure.

Which is probably why there are so many folk legends about the alleged difficulties of stopping, all those grim recitals of fearsome headaches and irresistible cravings . . .

'Bad tempered? He was like a grizzly bear with boils!'

For who doesn't like a protective cover-story about, er, only eventually giving in after a terrible struggle against impossible and overwhelming odds?

The battles we lose are traditionally harder fought than those we win, rearguard actions more heroic than swift advances.

Some of these 'failures' sink into fatalism, even fatality.

Some try again and again to stop, and keep on hoping despite all experience . . . with every new attempt ending deeper in the old guilt.

Some actually stop for the day, a week, a month, three months, a year . . . but one morning, noon, or night find themselves puffing away as though they'd never stopped.

What the Duke of Edinburgh can do . . .

The brutal truth is that you can't be 'cured', there's no miracle available from your friendly local supermarket, no strawberry-flavoured instant remedy to be taken three times a day after meals, no soothing balm to be applied with warm towels by somebody else.

Yes, somebody else can help — but only you can do it.

No book can help you to want to stop but, if you already want to, you can be helped to stop, and stay stopped.

Not so long ago the Duke of Edinburgh was 'smoking over fifty a day', and 'stopped abruptly'.

What he can do, anybody can do.

So what's stopping you from stopping?

Why not suck your thumb?

Probably the most compelling cause of smoking and reluctance to stop is smoking itself.

We live in a smoking world, where to smoke is still accepted as a typically ordinary activity. The cigarette (until only very recently) has usually been seen as merely another civilised adjunct to the Good Life: the car, the television, the twin-tub, the holiday abroad, the bottle of wine, the filter-tip king-size, the reflective pipe, the occasional cigar after dinner . . .

To smoke is to be known as a Man's Man, the mere inhaling of certain fumes recognised as a sign of masculinity, and for a woman to exhale through her dilated nostrils is a signal that she's one of the gang, every inch a sensuous female who knows how to handle herself. The pipe is a tribal mark of wisdom, much cherished by politicians who want to look like Elder

Statesmen for the cameras. The cigar is the badge of affluence and conspicuous expenditure.

Yet if a grown man sucked a dummy in public, or if a woman sucked her thumb, they'd be nudged about, even looked at curiously . . . suck a pipe or a cigarette, and what's there to look at?

The glass of fashion

It's helpful to remember that, not so long ago, it was also the 'done thing' for men and women to urinate and defecate in public.

The literature of seventeenth- and eighteenth-century England has many references to the custom. At dinners and parties, at the theatre, in taverns and coffee-houses, anywhere. Today it would be considered both a social and legal offence.

Again, 'snuffing' powdered tobacco was once the exquisite ritual of the born gentleman — while 'smoking' was quite out of fashion . . . only the 'low' or the 'fast' dared to risk anything quite so shockingly outrageous.

It was even at one time respectable to smoke in church during the sermon, as witness the churchwarden-pipe. Wonder what would happen today if you lit up during choral evensong in Westminster Abbey?

Such customs and fads and fashions and fancies change. . . .

* * *

Which means that the first small step towards stopping is to realise that there is nothing eternal about smoking. It is of comparatively recent origin . . . and the time is probably soon coming when it will go out of fashion again. It will be the unusual thing to smoke, and the men and women doing it will be seen as eccentrics, screwballs, committers of slow suicide — even as 'criminal' as drug addicts are today.

HOW TO STOP SMOKING

Yours it is to reason why

To stop smoking involves a radical change in your habits.

If you want to make such a change you'll need to understand the beginnings of that habit. Most smokers don't, preferring the self-forgiving dream to the likely embarrassment of truth.

But you've got to face the truth to understand precisely what you are trying to change: the nature and form of your habit.

And most smokers are at first surprised, then incredulous, then humiliated and ashamed, and finally relieved and encouraged to discover just how trivial the little bits and pieces of their habit can be when considered one by one . . . and how easy it is to change one small thing at a time.

You can empty the biggest bath ever made by pulling out one plug, stop the largest engine by cutting one wire . . . fill the darkest room with the light of one candle.

So *why* did you start to smoke?

*　　*　　*

Because you lived in a world of smokers?

You saw others smoking, parents, pastors and priests, teachers, most adults. You saw and heard cigarettes advertised, saw them on sale, were offered them, persuaded to smoke by your friends.

Yet you had to *learn* how to smoke, how to inhale without choking, how to control the coughing and spluttering caused by your first puffs, how to conceal the probable queasiness. Few smokers have ever enjoyed their early experiments. . . .

'I was sick as Monty Python's parrot for three days!'

So you must have co-operated, been willing and anxious to learn.

'All my mates smoked,' says the typical teenage boy, 'and I was the only one different. Tried a few, and soon got used to it.'

And many girls will admit that they started smoking for the same reasons they started using lipstick and eye-shadow: 'My friend offered me one, and I had a look at myself in her bedroom mirror — you know, standing there in an attitude like a model, and it made me look really something, experienced, like my friend. I must have been thirteen at the time. . . .'

Which is the cigarette as the key to the adult door. Or, to use the deadly jargon, 'peer pressures' . . . keeping up with the young Joneses. Yes, those pressures were real — but you *chose* to learn how to smoke rather than resist them.

So you can't blame the world, you can't blame other smokers, you can't blame the mere tempters: you actively helped yourself not to resist . . . *you* chose. . . .

And what began unpleasantly became just about tolerable, then perhaps a pleasure, still often or occasionally enjoyable . . . but is now more of a habit you hardly ever think about.

Yes, you may even think about its effects — you may even worry about them — but you've probably never examined all it is you're really doing when you reach for the packet.

In fact, you haven't got a Big Bad Habit, but lots and lots of little ones.

The Big 'Un can defeat you.

But who can't snap one matchstick?

You can't stop the world and get off

It's also worth remembering that you can't stop smoking by trying to change the smoking world — all you can do is make small changes in your own private corners.

And that will be enough.

Yes, you will have to avoid smokers as much as possible until you can say 'No' and mean it, do everything you can to understand why you 'need' to smoke at work.

Most of all you have to make sure that you know what pulls your particular trigger.

No, the safety-catch is merely useful — but it can be shifted, either deliberately or accidentally.

And other people can pull triggers.

So you've got to have such accurate self-knowledge that it

humiliates — and makes you laugh.

Because it's the smoking world you'll have to live in when you've stopped: you can't shelter for ever in your own small corner. And people will go on smoking, cigarettes will go on being advertised, being sold, they'll be offered to you, and even your friends may try to mock or tease or bully you into starting again.

We are all surrounded by the images of 'successful' smoking: ten thousand Heroes drag the smoke down into their lungs, flick the butt away in a casual arc, hitch their gun-belts, and then saunter out into Main Street to take on the entire Gallagher Gang singlehanded at High Noon . . . or the Universal Blonde in the tight black silk sheath dress flares her sensuous nostrils, parts her moist red lips, and allows the pale smoke to curl and coil and drift languorously upwards as she slowly, so very slowly, slides down the zipper . . .

Well, just remember Humphrey Bogart.

He could make a Big Drama of lighting a cigarette, fill the screen with menace by cupping his hands around the flame . . . or light two, and pass one to Lauren Bacall with a look that said more than any private eye could say with mere words . . .

'Down these mean streets a man must go who is not himself mean, who is neither tarnished nor afraid . . .'

Humphrey Bogart, who died of lung cancer, and became a legend, another statistic.

And remember that to kiss the blonde would be like kissing a damp ashtray.

Is there a life after smoke?

So please go on trying to understand . . . go on asking questions.

Do you think you started smoking because you genuinely felt you'd enjoy the experience? Or because you needed a 'lift' or a 'boost' or a 'fix' to cope with life?

Yes, how delightful that civilised luxury after a very good dinner, the satisfying little ritual of selecting the cigarette or the cigar, the management of the flame, the first slow breathing in of the cool smoke . . . the pleasure, the feeling of contentment, well-being . . . peace, perfect peace . . .

Or how necessary under the rush and tear of daily life to find some solace, some easing of tension in a quick cigarette: the bus or the train to catch, the work to be done, the job to be finished before five o'clock, delivery dates to meet, that blasted telephone always ringing . . . never enough time, never enough money, bills to pay, meals to cook, beds to make . . . people, kids, clatter . . .

'No, I simply couldn't cope without a smoke!'

Well, remember that you'll enjoy every pleasure so much more without smoking: food will taste better, wine will fill your mouth with untainted sunshine, kisses will be sweeter, loving will leave you gasping for all the right reasons.

And without a smokescreen you'll see your troubles more clearly, recognise them for what they are — never so bad in the light of morning . . . you'll have breath to run for that bus, be in charge of yourself, control your emotions when you need to, indulge them when you don't . . . you'll start to get rid of other psychological props and crutches . . . and you'll most certainly have more money to spare after you've paid those bills.

Read the small print first

So, yes, there are lots of good reasons why you should stop smoking as soon as possible . . . and we'll have a look at many more of them later on.

But there are also disadvantages — and you'd be unreasonable to ignore what it might mean.

True, they'll get fewer and fewer as you stay stopped for longer and longer . . . but, at first, you'll undoubtedly miss the pleasures of smoking: these are less intense and more intermittent than you now believe, but you'll miss them. You'll miss the company of your smoking friends for a while, some of the old familiar faces and places. You may feel a bit edgy or scratchy or irritable every so often for a couple or three days. You may lose your appetite entirely, or eat far too much, or fancy nothing but scrambled eggs or scampi-and-chips in the basket.

It's important to admit these as disadvantages, to know that stopping isn't going to be the flinging of roses, roses riotously all the way . . . otherwise you'll be unprepared when you start tripping over the snags.

For example, you'll experience mild withdrawal symptoms for a few days immediately after you stop: nothing very much, nothing you won't be able to manage in the same way as you get rid of an ordinary headache . . . but, obviously, you could do without any or all of these symptoms. Who needs a headache?

So accept it as a disadvantage, part of the small price you will have to pay for flushing the nicotine out of your system.

It's cost you a lot of time and money to get it in there . . . years and years, probably. What's a few hours?

Understand what's happening, and you can begin to regard these apparent disadvantages as signs of recovery rather than causes of misery: it's working . . . you're stopping.

* * *

There are also some other side-effects which aren't very often mentioned — not worth going on smoking for, but you're bound to notice that when your senses of taste and smell are back to normal there will be the occasional bad trips. Bad coffee tastes like bad coffee, plonk like diluted vinegar, cheap scent becomes a dead give-away, and people on crowded buses and trains most certainly don't smell of morning-gathered dew-fresh violets.

But that's life and the living of it . . . and all you have to do is think of all that good coffee to come, the promise of that small bottle of something a bit special chilling in the refrigerator, the perfume that lingers with insidious intent, the healthy glow of flesh warm from the bath . . .

As always, balance the books.

And go on understanding . . .

2

What Sort of Smoker are You?

To understand your own smoking habits is the second small step towards stopping, and to know what sort of smoker you are is to answer some questions about ways and means before they're asked.

Many of us can answer all manner of difficult questions: the trick is for somebody to ask the right ones.

*   *   *

It's possible to describe a number of typical smokers, though human beings are not 'types' but people . . . and the only thing you can really stuff into a neat and tidy pigeon-hole is a dead pigeon. So these categories are admittedly rough and ready: signposts towards stopping, not police 'Wanted' notices.

You and the part you are playing

Some people are Social Smokers: they're not smoking from deep physical need or craving, but putting on some sort of public or even private performance. They're acting the Man of their own day-dreams, or the Sophisticate, or the Sex Goddess, or whoever.

All those Bogart-lightings in cupped hands and eyes puckered against the smoke curling up from the king-size drooping at the lips, all those long amber holders and gold bands and Balkan blends and fastidious tappings of ash, all those seductive fingerings and gentle smoothings and delicate tip-of-the-tongue touchings of what is only after all a cigarette . . . all these mean something to the smoker: they are signs and signals by which they want to be known, as much part of the uniform of recognition as their badges and stickers and football scarves and old school ties and message-printed T-shirts.

In the South Seas it's a bone through the nose, or a crimson flower tucked behind the left ear: in contemporary Britain it's how you handle your cigarette.

You've seen them, these self-describing smokers: the Wise Old Author with his faithful briar-pipe and cocker spaniel, the Sensitive Connoisseur of first editions with his slim cigar and cut-glass tumbler of twelve-year-old malt whisky, the Posy Simmonds Sociology Lecturer in a duffle coat rolling his or her own . . . the Hard-boiled Reporter, the Boxing Promoter, the Woman Executive as played by Faye Dunaway . . . the Mississippi Gambler, the Con from Cell Block A . . . the Shop Steward . . .

Stereotypes?

Whatever they are, they're not smokers in the addicted sense.

True, they might be unable to stop — but they are probably smoking for other and more important reasons (to them) than mere nicotine. Yes, all smokers get some satisfactions from these social and ritual aspects, from displaying their mastery of the cigarette and the necessary equipment — just as these acting smokers get some physical pleasure from the smoke . . . but they are separate and distinct activities.

And it helps to know what you are trying to change: your dependence on the smoke or the part you are playing.

So, are you playing a part? And in what play?

And why do you need to be playing any part at all? Why are you acting? What's wrong with who you really are? Do you even know much more about yourself than your name and address and marital status? Might you be smoking because of what you don't know?

All you've got to do is stop fiddling

Fiddling Smokers are slightly different: they also make a big performance of their mastery over the cigarette and all the bits and bobs of necessary equipment . . . but for other reasons.

They're always adjusting the flame on the lighter, or fussing with the flint, or the wick, or the fuel, testing to make sure that everything still works . . . or they do all sorts of fascinating things with spent matches, breaking them into a certain number of pieces before dropping them into the ashtray, or arranging them carefully in a row or a pattern on the table, or sharpening one end and picking their teeth or cleaning their nails . . . or they have special ways of flicking or tapping or blowing off the ash . . . or of holding the cigarette between fingers like an American or a Frenchman or an Italian, rolling or sliding or twirling . . . always on the move, playing with this or toying with that, opening and shutting the packet, making stars or flowers or tiny cups with the silver paper . . .

Yes, they'd be better off playing with real toys: if they asked themselves the right questions they'd be fiddling with wire-puzzles, or making scale models of vintage cars, or learning how to touch-type, or caressing a small jewel or curiously shaped stone . . .

What's smoking got to do with what they're doing?

You and your Rolls-Royce

Leisure Smokers are those you see in the glossy advertisements, *Penthouse* or *Cosmo* or the Sunday Colour Supplements: laid back, relaxed and real cool, enhancing their pleasures with a civilised luxury. They've got simple good taste, enough money to afford nothing but the best, all the time in the world to enjoy early Bach or late Beiderbecke, to lean casually against the Rolls or lounge by the side of the pool . . .

'Let's celebrate.'

'Celebrate what, darling?'

'Does it matter?'

Well, these smokers aren't really smoking, either — merely going through the exquisite motions. If the 'leisure' thing to be doing these days was sniffing fastidiously at a pomander or an orange spiked with cloves, that's what they'd be doing.

Smoking's got little or nothing to do with it.

Of course you don't necessarily have to have a private income to be a Leisure Smoker: it's not how much money you've got, but how you see yourself . . . and the most leisured smoker I've ever known was a man sleeping rough underneath the arches at Charing Cross, who scrounged a couple of bob for a cup of tea — and taught me a lesson in the sheer enjoyment of a fag-end. That man would have enjoyed a wet Sunday afternoon on the wrong end of Cromer Pier.

Which is the secret of more than how to stop smoking: enjoy the pleasure for itself, squeeze out the last little drop of juice . . . and who needs to 'enhance' the already delectable?

Running up the down escalator

Some smokers smoke to start the engine, to get going, to keep going, to force themselves to go faster or further, to last the course, not slow down, stay up with the leaders, ride over the next rough patch, reach the light at the end of the tunnel, the drive back at the end of the day, then the evening, a few friends, a few drinks, a million laughs . . . and then the night, the night, the night . . . and then the morning . . .

To stop smoking, such smokers have to stop a lot more . . . because if the smoking don't get 'em, the pressure must.

So their need to smoke is merely the special case of their larger problem: stop the smoking, stop the running, slow down . . . for smoking is not the only way to ask for a heart attack.

The fag as friend

Other smokers need a friend: comes grief, comes sorrow, bad news or a rainy day, the Final Demand in red, the rent, the rates, the Income Tax, or the cat's messed on the carpet, there's a black cloud across the sun, blood on the moon, the

WHAT SORT OF SMOKER ARE YOU?

car's in dock, short time at work, no prospects, that tooth needs filling . . .

'I've had enough, I've had it up to here!'

Well, at times like that a cigarette comes easier than a friend, because all you've got to do is light it.

Though wouldn't a friend or a lover still be there even though you smoked through the packet? And which would you rather have? A person to listen or a full ashtray to empty?

So, again, smoking is the special case of a larger problem: make a friend, and you'll have somebody to help you stop smoking. Understand why you need to smoke, and you'll see your need for a friend. And the best way to make a friend is to be friendly, to listen to somebody else's troubles, come grief, come sorrow. . . .

Ever had two at once?

Habitual Smokers have little problem in stopping, because they hardly notice when they're smoking at all.

Mind you, they hardly ever notice when they're not!

Been at it for donkey's years, rarely given it a thought . . .

'Well, it's not anything that needs much thought, is it?'

Always got a cigarette on the go somewhere: smoking it, holding it, smouldering in the ashtray . . . somewhere . . .

Sometimes burns away, and they wonder where it's gone. Or they light one in the loo, and find they've still got one on the edge of the draining-board in the kitchen . . . or they're reading, and reach for the packet — and there's one in their other hand . . .

'Not often — but, well, yes, it *has* happened a few times.'

Few smokers will readily admit that they pay so much for so little conscious enjoyment. . . .

But once they've seen what they're actually doing, once they've become aware of the real nature of their habit, these are the smokers who find it easiest to stop. After all, there's little they have to stop: a series of reflex actions, a habit almost without content. Can't really call it smoking!

'You've Come a Long Way, Baby!'

The woman who smokes as a sign of 'liberation' should have even less of a problem: all she has to do is realise that her smoking is merely one of the ways she's trying to be as 'free' as a man.

'Look, Mum, I'm really a boy!'

Many people are all for equality between the sexes, and honest men will readily admit that women have usually had (and are still having) a rough deal in our man-dominated society — but what has smoking like a man got to do with the freedom to be a woman? For if she sees herself as no man's slave, why should she need the same master as so many men?

One American company actually produces slightly shorter and thinner cigarettes specifically designed for the 'free-striding and decision-making woman of today's world'. With calculated shrewdness, these are called 'Slims' . . . thus pandering to the alleged 'slender femininity' of a woman's 'natural' self-image. Their advertising slogan, which adds insult to cancer, speaks directly to the 'emancipated' customer: 'You've Come a Long Way, Baby' . . . as though to smoke like a man is progress for a woman, and to be called 'Baby' is anything but patronising, even patriarchal.

Are you a nicotine junkie?

The Heavy Smoker is the one with problems.

Not all that much to do with the number of cigarettes smoked in a day, though it tends to be large, more than forty, often fifty or more — but it's the seriousness of the smoking that matters: there's a recognisable quality about it, a sense of urgency, even desperation . . . true need, chemical dependence.

Addiction . . .

Which is a loaded and emotive word, a nastier fact, and a very difficult truth to admit about yourself.

Especially to yourself.

WHAT SORT OF SMOKER ARE YOU?

But if you get less and less from smoking more and more, if you're coughing a lot and it worries you, if the stairs are getting steeper and higher and your breath shorter, if you've got pains in your legs and your heart is obviously not what it used to be . . . if you'd like to stop smoking and know you can't — then please go to a doctor the first thing tomorrow morning.

You're an addict.

Spike Milligan put it starkly years ago: 'Cigarette smokers who can't stop are really nicotine junkies who cannot kick the habit. They are drug addicts.'

Even the thought might be enough to stop you.

But to accept it as true will at least convince you that you're going to need all the help you can get to stop. It's worse than useless to tinker with an addiction — you've got to take it very seriously. Though even the heroin junkie can be helped to stop.

You're not an addict?

If you have to smoke before you can get out of bed in the morning, if you have to smoke before you can sleep at night, you're an addict.

Though there's a lot of help available, and a lot you can do to help yourself.

Yes, you can stop.

You, too, can do the impossible

In stopping, you won't be alone.

Since the early 1960s, when the dangers of smoking began to be widely known, nine million people have stopped . . . and what they can do, you can do.

Many of them say that they 'found it surprisingly easy'.

Even in wanting to stop, or merely being interested in the possibility of stopping, you're in good company — because most smokers say they'd like to.

Mind you, it's been pointed out by some shrewd observers that many smokers who try are 'merely seeking to prove to themselves that it's impossible'.

Which is really to say: 'If I, of all people, can't stop, it must be impossible — I *can't* stop, so, therefore, it is indeed impossible. Which means that I can't be blamed for failing.'

Put that way, it's less convincing.

One smoker dies every five minutes

To stop, you've got to stop making excuses.

And you've got to do it yourself. You were probably helped over your first few cigarettes, and you'll almost certainly need some help with your last few . . . but the choice is always yours.

And though you'll get all the help you need, you mustn't rely on other people — if necessary you must go it alone.

Because it remains a smoking world.

Which means that dying from tobacco is a fact of life in it.

Yes, we've all heard of somebody who smoked sixty a day for eighty-seven years, and lived to be a hundred and three.

But the brutal fact is that two thousand British people die from tobacco every week . . . about three hundred a day . . . twelve an hour . . . say one every five minutes.

It's only as you die that you believe it can happen to you.

The choice is always yours.

You could make it now.

How to become a statistic

Please remember that tobacco is different.

If you drink, it's possible not to be an alcoholic . . . delightful to enjoy the occasional glass of wine or beer or cider.

Drinking can be safe for you.

Because alcohol gives its own immediate warning: drink too much, and you're drunk.

So total abstinence isn't the only option.

Smoke too much, smoke at all, and it'll be years before you

WHAT SORT OF SMOKER ARE YOU?

start to notice the results.

Wait a few more years, and you'll be a statistic.

* * *

Another thought before starting your stopping.

A good friend of mine who works as a floor-sweeper in a factory has noticed how most smokers flick their stubs as far from themselves as possible, into corners, behind radiators, out of sight, anywhere, only so long as they can't see them.

Out of mind?

Are they trying to say something?

To themselves?

3

Ways of Stopping

There are many ways available by means of which smokers can stop smoking, though not all of them will appeal to everybody. Different people are convinced by different reasons, persuaded by different arguments, moved by different emotions, driven by different motives.

Indeed, some apparently conclusive reasons may merely reinforce the psychological pattern of resistance to change.

For example, if one sort of smoker learns of the genuine disgust experienced by many non-smokers in the presence of what they regard as an addict, it might confirm the resolution to stop. . . .

'Must have been really terrible for my wife all these years.'

Or it might induce deeper feelings of self-doubt and unworthiness: 'If that's what they think — well, what the Hell does it matter whether I live or die?' And the next cigarette is lit from the half-smoked stub of the present one.

* * *

If you are a Heavy Smoker test yourself, examine your feelings: What's your immediate reaction to this?

A non-smoker has just told you that he loathes all smokers, especially women, and that it takes the full strength of mind he can muster not to blast off at the utterly selfish coughing and spitting and spluttering and defiling of fresh air which you weak-willed drug addicts inflict on the rest of us. You are ash-smeared, finger-stained, fur-tongued, foul-breathed, lung-rotted, smelly, probably impotent . . . and anyway about as sexually desirable as the bottom of a sick parrot's cage . . .

Agreed, such overstatement spoils the case — but you may be so ashamed that you'll stop here and now.

Though I doubt it.

You'll probably cringe a bit inside, have a pang or two of

WAYS OF STOPPING

guilt, shrug . . . and reach for the packet.

You just don't see yourself that way at all. To use the jargon: it 'contradicts the reality of your self-image'.

In the opinion of many smokers (and lots of other people) most such militant non-smokers are obviously touched, forever given to old-fashioned Evangelical misery. They are the Nay-sayers, the men in black suits and sincere smiles, Total Abstainers from all manner of pleasures, Puritans . . . and their condemnations are ineffectual.

Even to point out in a restrained way some of the dangers to health doesn't always make people stop. Ever since the lung cancer 'scares' of the 1960s a series of Medical Officers of Health have noted that the 'abolition of cigarette-smoking would be the greatest single contribution to public health now open to us'. And they have devised some arresting ways of presenting their facts and figures: 'During the last six years tobacco has killed twice as many British people as were killed during the Second World War.'

And millions of British people go on smoking.

'In Britain,' say the Official Voices, 'tobacco kills four times as many people as the total killed by drink, drugs, murder, suicide, road accidents, rail accidents, poisoning, drowning, fires, falls, snakes, lightning, and every other known cause of accidental death all put together.'

And those tens of millions still go on. . . .

True, nine million fewer than used to . . . but such unarguable facts and deadly figures ought to have stopped the lot where they stood: that should have been the end of the tobacco industry.

Obviously not: one person's cancer may be another person's reason for stopping . . . while some would smoke at the funeral.

So remember that not all (if any) reasons are compelling, and that only some of the ways of stopping may suit you.

*   *   *

There are two main groups of ways: one relying on your own

inner resources, the other on external techniques.

Sweet reason

The first is simple, direct, and often highly effective.

All you need to do is consider the various reasons for stopping. Once persuaded that one is compelling enough, then the mere force of reason may be all you need. You won't have to use any of the techniques, or change your pattern of life very much — but will have stopped, as easy as that.

Yet even if the reason isn't compelling, and you've got to change your life and habits in various ways, it's still extremely important that you should understand why you want to stop smoking: that you should be convinced you ought to stop.

Most smokers are already slightly uneasy about smoking, even though they go on: 'Of course,' they say, 'we could if we wanted to, we will if we really have to — so what do we have to prove?'

Which is a good enough start to build on.

But the hardening of this slight unease into a determination is undoubtedly the most difficult part of the entire process. Given that determination, the mere 'how' of stopping is of relatively minor importance — for when the total resources of your character are used there is very little which is actually impossible by way of change for the better.

And about a third of moderate or even heavy smokers find it comparatively easy to stop . . . once convinced of their need.

*   *   *

Some of the most convincing reasons are those related to health.

True, it's often counter-productive to try to frighten yourself into stopping by brooding on those chilling facts and figures.

People have stopped after seeing one of the films in which a blackened and cancerous lung is cut out, or after seeing gobbets of their own tar-smeared phlegm. Others have lit a cigarette to steady their nerves.

'And figures can be made to prove anything, can't they?'

Which demonstrates that physiology isn't enough: to stop smoking is at least as much a psychological problem.

It's not the cigarette, it's you

Because more is involved than merely the stopping of your smoking: your whole life and style as a person is questioned.

To stop the smoking you'll be changing your habits, your view of the world, your attitudes to people, some of your pleasures . . . and you have to start accepting full responsibility for yourself and for your life.

Now take another test, examine your feelings again: What's your immediate reaction to these next assertions:

Like it or not, until you stop smoking you are shifting some of this responsibility from yourself to cigarettes — it's not the real you that's doing the living, but a distorted less-than-you as stimulated or tranquillised by nicotine.

Until you stop smoking your pleasures are so modified that they often cease to be pleasurable.

There are some people who actually prevent you from smoking when and where you want to . . . all these non-smoking compartments and special seats in cinemas and restaurants . . . no knowing where it will end.

'Glad enough of our taxes, aren't they?'

And until you stop smoking you can hardly be said to have had a clear view of the world: the smoke's been getting in your eyes.

And as for your habits . . .

Which is to question, as threatened, your whole life and style.

Well, are they mere assertions?

Do you reject them?

If so, why do you reject them? Do they make you feel irritable? Are you resentful at being described in such terms? At having your character assassinated? Isn't it like that at all?

Whatever your answers, even if you admit that some of it

might possibly be true, I hope that you were involved enough to spark just a little bit, to defend your present values and choices, to want to argue . . . because such a response will tell you better than I could that there are psychological pressures under the surface: pressures which started you smoking, keep you smoking . . . and which must be used to stop you smoking.

*　　*　　*

Easier said than done.

You have to switch off the dream-machine, give over kidding yourself, accept yourself for what you are rather than what you imagine yourself to be.

You have to wake up to reality . . . and 'human kind cannot bear very much reality'.

To go on smoking is to go on dreaming . . . the dream in which we floor the lout with a single karate blow, or wait in soft-focus on the balcony as our lover climbs the ivy . . .

The trouble with the dreams of smoke is that they so often slowly fade into nightmares.

Doctor, doctor . . .

Because the medical facts are there, and are not disputed except by the desperate.

- Tobacco contains up to three per cent of nicotine, a drug which will in small amounts stimulate or tranquillise you, in larger doses harm you, and in slightly larger ones kill you.

Inject the nicotine of a single cigarette straight into the bloodstream of a full-grown healthy man, and he's dead. It's so strong a poison that it's widely used to destroy insects impervious to other poisons.

Why smoke insecticide?

- About five per cent of cigarette smoke is carbon monoxide, the same stuff that billows out of car exhausts . . . and some suicides use to kill themselves.

Unless you intend to commit suicide, why join them?

- The yellow-brown tars in cigarette smoke cause cancer in small animals: some tars are thought to start the formation of various malignities, some stimulate them to more rapid growth.

If you smeared the stuff around your eyes, or up your nose, or all over your lips, you'd be . . .

Well, what would you call yourself?

So why dribble it down your throat into your lungs?

- There are several other dangerous substances in cigarette smoke, including the base ingredients of the bleaches used in sink and lavatory cleaners. Ever thought of taking a swig?

Hydrogen cyanide . . . 'which,' says Miriam Stoppard, 'appears at concentrations more than one-hundred-and fifty times those considered safe in industry'.

And *phenol*, a solvent, 'which is corrosive, poisonous, and a severe irritant'.

Or do you regard yourself, alone among men, unique of all women, as invulnerable? Able to catch bullets in your teeth?

*   *   *

Smoke twenty a day, and you shorten your life by five years.

Or, to put it another way, the cigarette that takes five minutes to smoke takes five minutes from your life, a packet of ten costs nearly an hour, and twenty most of an evening with your Beloved . . .

'I've got to leave you now, darling, but I'm on my way to an early grave.'

*   *   *

'The evidence is now incontrovertible,' says Doctor Henry Miller, 'that the cigarette is the main cause of the present epidemic of lung cancer, the steady toll of which is comparable in its magnitude with that of such infections of the past as cholera, typhoid, and tuberculosis. Cigarette smoking is also a major cause of chronic bronchitis and emphysema, with its years of distressing breathlessness, and its ultimately high mortality. It is a major contributory factor in the increasing death rate from coronary thrombosis, as well as in the diffuse arterial degeneration that gradually closes the arteries of the lower limbs, and characteristically makes walking at first agonisingly painful, and ultimately impossible. I have had patients and friends, each of whom suffered from every one of these complications of heavy smoking — chronic bronchitis, general arterial disease, and cancer of the lung, during the course of which illness they were carried off by coronary thrombosis.'

Smoking before birth

There are additional risks if you are a woman.

'A woman should give up smoking for her own sake,' says Miriam Stoppard, 'and the desire to have a healthy child demands that she gives up smoking during pregnancy.'

It harms the foetus, 'spontaneous abortion is more common', the 'mortality rates are higher and the birth rate is lower', there are 'more still-births', the 'incidence of prematurity' is 'almost double', the baby will be born weighing less than it ought to, and there are 'more deaths in the first week of life'.

And Miriam Stoppard is not only a doctor, but a mother.

'Infants and young children whose parents smoke,' says the Royal College of Physicians, 'get more chest infections and pneumonia than those whose parents do not smoke.'

And, by the age of eleven, the children of smoking mothers tend to be shorter, clumsier, and less good at reading and other school work . . . and will probably be smokers themselves in two years.

*   *   *

There's too much published evidence to ignore: you can either stop smoking . . . or stop reading.

WAYS OF STOPPING

Tomorrow never comes

However, it must be admitted that such apparently conclusive arguments are often quite useless.

Because the worst effects of smoking do not appear for many years, and the remote possibilities of resultant illness or early death rarely deter. Put a bullet into a gun, point the gun at your head, squeeze the trigger — and that's that. But put a cigarette between your lips, puff away — and you'll need to go on puffing for ten or twelve years to work up the beginnings of a crippling case of chronic bronchitis or emphysema . . . and it takes several years longer for your lungs to rot or your heart to stop.

Who lives that far into the future?

'I'd sooner smoke myself to death than sit around waiting for the nuclear holocaust. What's there to choose?'

And knowledge isn't always everything . . .

Well over three-quarters of all smokers continue to smoke despite knowing about the established connexions with these diseases.

And a spokesman for the tobacco industry agrees: 'Smokers know the dangers of smoking, and have not given it up. There is no reason to believe they will.'

He has hundreds of thousands of reasons for his confidence, all of them sick, dying, or dead smokers.

For example, as pointed out by Doctor Miller, smoking causes peripheral vascular disease, or constriction of the arteries of the arms and legs, which sometimes leads to permanent damage and eventual amputation. Well, incredibly, many of these smokers continue to smoke after their amputations, even when they're told that it could well cost them the other leg. And there's the famous case of the man who had both legs amputated, went on smoking, and died within the month from a heart attack.

* * *

Not that the arguments are all on the one side . . . for the tobacco industry has its spokesmen and defenders.

For example, it has been maintained that as most people in the medically protected Western world are no longer dying from the traditional killer diseases in early life, they are now living to the greater ages when other diseases can kill them. The very success of medical science is thus preserving people for diseases which they never lived long enough to suffer and die from before.

So, apparently, it used to be cholera at birth, diphtheria at ten, and typhus during your early teens . . . and is now bronchitis, cancer, and coronary thrombosis as you live longer — whether you smoke or not.

A similar line of defence is that our generally higher standard of living, with its rich food, readily available alcohol, and lack of physical exercise, brings with it the newer diseases of self-indulgence and excess.

And the spokesmen have also suggested another explanation of what seems to be the fact that heavy smokers are twenty times more likely to die of lung cancer than non-smokers. This is 'merely a statistical association', and 'does not prove a cause-and-effect relationship between smoking and lung cancer'.

In my opinion you'd need to own shares in the tobacco companies to take such arguments very seriously.

Yet I'm not merely offering them as straw-men to demolish, but as illustrations of the psychological defence mechanisms called into action when any of our cherished interests, opinions, values, habits, or vices are questioned. We all share these mechanisms (you should just see my elaborate system) . . . and it takes more than any direct frontal attack to get through — more than words.

The handkerchief test

One very simple way of persuading yourself about the strength of these medical reasons for stopping is to breathe smoke through a clean white handkerchief. Once, that's all . . . and then look at the smudge of pale yellow gunge: a lethal mixture of tars, known poisons, and irritants.

You not only inhale it hundreds of times a day, but it remains in your body, slowly clogging and corroding . . .

Is that what you want?

You decarbonise your car or motorbike every few thousand miles, yet deliberately carbonise your lungs.

Are you worth less care and maintenance than a mere engine?

Go on, get a clean white handkerchief . . .

Twenty cigarettes a day, and you're puffing that lot into yourself a hundred thousand times a year.

The power of positive non-smoking

However, don't make the mistake of being negative about any of these medical considerations.

Yes, smoking is undoubtedly a serious danger to health: if cigarettes were to be newly invented, and the manufacturers tried to put them on the market, they'd be banned.

In all probability, if there wasn't so much money to be made from them, so much government revenue from taxes, they'd already be banned . . . or their use would at least be tightly controlled.

But to stop smoking is not simply to say 'No' to ill-health and premature death. Rather, it's a positive action, a decisive move towards a more richly rewarding life.

Yes, you'll be healthier, fitter, have an improved sense of well-being . . . but you'll also be a self-reliant human being.

To stop smoking isn't the end of anything you need regret, but the beginning of something you'll enjoy until the day you die: your new life.

You won't only be stopping, but starting.

So please don't feel pressured or threatened. Unless you choose freely, it's hardly a choice. And stopping is mostly about choosing, about you as a responsible person making your own daily decisions, living your own way in your own time.

Besides, the medical facts merely describe the long-term

consequences of smoking.

We are now concerned with the short-term benefits of stopping.

And not so much stopping as succeeding.

Did Jesus roll his own?

For some Christians who smoke the appeal to Christian principles might be enough to stop them.

'Don't you know that you are the Temple of God?' wrote Paul to the Christians in Corinth, 'and that the Spirit of God lives in you? God will surely destroy any man who defiles His Holy Temple — which is exactly what you are! Never forget that your body is the Temple of the Holy Spirit, and that you are not your own to do what you like with.'

To the Christian such considerations could be conclusive.

True, most preachers seem to concentrate on the sexual aspects of keeping this Temple 'clean and pure', but the heart and lungs are just as much a part of our bodies as our genitals.

So, advises Paul, just as we are to keep our bodies clean on the outside, so also should we keep our insides clean.

If we would not deliberately smear ourselves with filth or tar or dangerous chemical waste, why should we inhale such filth into ourselves? Is the skin more the work of God than the guts?

If we brush our teeth two or three times a day, and visit the dentist every six months to keep them in good condition, why stain them with corrosive smoke? Why risk cancer of the gums?

If we eat good wholesome food to stay alive and healthy, why ingest a lethal drug which will make us unhealthy, shorten life, and cause us to become a burden on others?

In more emotional words: How can a smoke-blackened slum be any sort of Temple for the Holy Spirit?

Again, if Christians are supposed to have free and open access to Jesus Christ, the very source of life, and that 'more abundantly', what need should they have for nicotine?

Can you see Jesus Christ smoking?
Not thirsting on the Cross, but craving?

Wine, roses, and kisses

For other smokers, with an interest in the pleasures of the body and its senses, it might be enough to realise that professional wine-tasters do not smoke. It injures the delicate mucous membranes of the nose, mouth, and throat, and would thus make it impossible for them to distinguish the aromas, the bouquets, the sweetness or the dryness of various wines and vintages.

And this also applies to the other pleasures of the palate: if you smoke, your full enjoyment of all but the most highly-spiced food is impaired, even spoiled.

How long is it since you noticed the perfume of a rose? No, not by the dozen in the florists or on the market-stall, but one by one, bush by bush, out there in the garden, first thing of a Summer morning? 'The wild thyme unseen and the wild strawberry . . .'

Stop smoking . . . and fresh air is more invigorating, kisses are sweeter, and orgasms are more overwhelming.

Who can soar to the heights of sexual loving while struggling for breath? Or worried about a heart attack?

Don Juan and forty a day

The effects of smoking on sexual 'performance' are not at all as promised by the advertisements.

A Medical Correspondent, Oliver Gillie, recently described the results of some studies made by a group of French doctors, as reported in *The Lancet*.

'Impotence is most commonly caused by poor blood circulation, brought on in middle-age by smoking and a diet high in fat', and it may be 'reversed, or at least arrested, by giving up cigarettes and improving the diet'.

And, as we shall see, part of the process of stopping involves modifying your diet in favour of lighter and fresher foods.

It used to be thought that impotence was 'all in the mind', caused by anxiety or stress, but now it's been found that 'eight out of ten cases result from damage to blood vessels', which 'reduces blood pressure in the penis'. Even a 'small constriction to the artery inside the penis' is enough to 'prevent erection'. A similar constriction 'causes coronary heart disease', and (as we have already seen) those amputations of the legs.

Men whose impotence was 'caused by poor circulation' were 'twice as likely to be smokers'.

These findings 'are a blow for tobacco manufacturers,' wrote Oliver Gillie, because they have always 'promoted smoking as sexy and macho . . .'

But even without the disappointments and frustrations of male impotence, it can't always be pleasant to make love with a smoker: the constant smell of stale smoke, the stained fingers, the yellowed teeth . . . the bad breath . . .

Burning fivers

Another very simple way of persuading yourself about the costs of smoking is to burn money.

Yes, there are obviously many social costs, but never forget just how much real money you spend.

So go on, take a crisp new five-pound note, strike a match, and light the hard-earned thing rather than a cigarette. You could even try sniffing at the smoke, which has a strangely distinctive smell — something to do with the printing ink . . .

You can't bring yourself to do anything quite so silly?

Well, remind yourself: That's what you're actually doing when you smoke — not quite so quickly, perhaps, but inevitably.

At present prices (certain to increase as the years pass and Budgets spiral upwards), if you smoke twenty a day you spend just under a tenth of the average weekly wage on . . . what?

If you started at the age of fifteen or sixteen, and reached thirty a day by your fortieth birthday, you'll have spent ten or twelve years of your wages by the time you retire at sixty-five . . . if you live that long.

So you pay the price of a small house for a case of lung cancer, seven or eight new cars for an early death from chronic bronchitis, and forty annual holidays abroad for a probably fatal attack of coronary thrombosis.

And most of that money goes on taxation and the vast costs of advertising campaigns designed to persuade smokers to smoke more, or even merely to change brands.

It would be much less harmful, and certainly just as sensible, to strike that match and burn the fiver.

Be a happy miser

But, again, don't make the mistake of being negative — because to stop smoking is not simply to stop spending money, but a positive way of using your money to better effect. And all it costs is a resolution which will be easier to keep the longer you keep it. After the first few days or weeks you'll hardly notice that you're keeping anything . . . except your money.

- Some people save what they would otherwise have spent on a packet, and put the pound note or the coins into a piggy bank or box or tin . . . or, better still, in a large glass jar up on a shelf or the mantelpiece where they can see and be reminded just how much they've been spending all these years.
- Others work out the price of one cigarette, and put the pennies aside every time they feel the temptation and resist.
- And others calculate the cost for a week or a month, and bank that amount in a savings account.

The point is that you should make yourself realise exactly how much you actually spend on cigarettes . . . and the probable shock may shame you into stopping.

Who could possibly burn all that real money?

'Perhaps,' says Miriam Stoppard, 'it's a habit you can no longer afford. Think what you would do with the money you could save . . . the first things that you would spend your savings on.'

HOW TO STOP SMOKING

Are you really sure you're smoking?

If you keep an accurate account of how many cigarettes you actually smoke a day, as opposed to how many you think you do, or admit to other people, you'll probably be surprised.

It's so easy to take your smoking for granted, and most smokers tend to underestimate. . . .

'You know,' they'll say, 'about a packet.'

A packet of ten?

'Well, no, twenty . . . a packet of twenty.'

But if they start counting, making a note of each cigarette as they lit it, they'd likely find that they have one when they wake up or get out of bed in the morning, one before breakfast, one after, a couple on the way to work, one when they arrive, a couple or three during the morning, one with their coffee, a couple during the rest of the morning, one before lunch, a couple after, another couple before tea, one after, then a couple more, more on the way home, more if they call in at their local for a drink . . .

That's over twenty before they've started on the evening.

So it's important to be honest with yourself, because you're the easiest person to kid.

But if you can be humiliatingly honest, and then establish how many of these cigarettes you really enjoy, as opposed to how many you merely smoke for habit or association of ideas . . .

'I always have one with my coffee.'

Well, you'll almost certainly be more than surprised.

- How many do you look forward to? Light up with conscious pleasure? Smoke to the last slow luxurious puff? And remember for longer than a few minutes?
- And how many make you cough and splutter and leave you with a nasty taste? How many do you find yourself smoking without being fully aware of having lit them? Have you ever lit one, and then noticed another still half-smoked in the ashtray? Do you stub one out after a few puffs, and then light another within a few minutes? If you were blindfolded, would

you really be quite sure that the cigarette you were 'smoking' was really burning?

And don't be too indignant until it's been tried on you, for hundreds and hundreds of even heavy smokers have been caught out by this simple experiment: you're blindfolded, somebody lights two out of three cigarettes, and puts them into your mouth one after the other . . . you aren't allowed to touch them, just puff away at each for as long as you like, then it's changed for another, then another . . . until you've had a go at each one at least three times. And then you're asked which two were lit, and which one wasn't. Or even if any were lit at all.

And what you may not notice is that none of them is alight, or that all three are . . . and there you'll be, happily choosing, happily telling the difference, and happily making a fool of yourself.

In other words: how many cigarettes do you smoke, as opposed to the cigarettes that smoke you? How many are an unmitigated pleasure? How many do you hardly experience at all?

The question then becomes: why do you have to smoke so many in order to enjoy so few?

Even stubbing out one cigarette half-smoked is a waste of money. Why buy twice as many as you actually smoke? Or perhaps as many as ten times as those you really enjoy?

Imagine doing that in a pub . . .

'Ten pints, please, and pour nine straight down the sink.'

Or in a restaurant on your next evening out . . .

'Seven of your Set Dinners . . . and a large swill-bin.'

The smoker's guide to simple arson

Another reason for not smoking is that smokers tend to be more accident-prone than non-smokers.

For one thing, they're always playing with fire.

Over a third of all accidental fires in Britain are caused by careless smokers: the butt is left smouldering on the edge of a table or desk or bench, or flicked away into a heap of rags or wood-shavings, or dropped into a bin full of paper or plastic . . . and up goes the shop or the office or the factory or the club. . . . And every year there are probably hundreds of people who burn down their own homes: usually starts in the cushions of an easy chair, or the bedclothes . . . and they injure themselves, their families, sometimes seriously . . . sometimes fatally. . . .

And smokers have higher accident rates at work, have more days off through sickness . . . and often behave in ways which would baffle the most intelligent Extra-Terrestrial. For example, in some factories you can see men wearing industrial masks to protect themselves against fumes which are far less dangerous to health than the cigarettes they take off their masks to smoke.

Even stranger is the fact that by taking off their masks they are breaking the law designed for their safety — though there aren't any laws to protect them against smoking.

*   *   *

Those, then, have been some of the more obvious reasons for you to stop smoking . . . the idea being that the mere force of reason may be all you need. No smoker will be able to stop unless there's a sufficiently compelling reason — which usually requires a firm resolution to back it, a determination to success, a willingness to admit even the worst truth about yourself . . . to yourself.

But for many smokers this is not enough: they need detailed guidance, practical support, a technique for stopping . . . more than a principle or a general way: they need external means, a method . . . almost a set of instructions.

However, before going on to consider these, there are a few other ways open to smokers who are capable of stopping by their own unaided efforts . . . merely by calling upon the powers of the mind, using their own inner resources.

4

Using the Mind to Stop

One deceptively simple way of stopping is to understand why you smoke at all: to ask and answer some innocent-sounding questions to help you realise what your true 'need' is.

As with the reasons for stopping, when to be persuaded or convinced by them may have been enough, so with understanding the real nature of your need: to see (perhaps for the first time) what you're really doing, and to admit to yourself why you're doing it, may well be the exhilarating revelation of self-knowledge that will douse your last cigarette.

At the very least it will help you to choose the best method of stopping, the one most suitable for your own particular character and circumstances.

Whatever you do, don't rationalise, don't invent fancy excuses, but face yourself with (perhaps) humiliating honesty.

Your answers to these questions, if honest, should provide you with some valuable information about the pattern of your habit.

Once you've recognised this pattern, seen it for what it is, you are well on the way to altering it. Because, almost invariably, your real reasons for smoking are not what you either believe or pretend them to be.

So bring them out into the sunshine, and see if they can stand in the light without cringing.

Nicotine or the nipple?

When you smoke, what are you sucking?

Some psychiatrists claim that smoking, especially a pipe or a large cigar, has elements of the oral gratification enjoyed by the suckling infant: that the pipe or cigar is a substitute for the bottle or nipple.

The baby suckles, the adult smokes.

There's no need to follow these seductive pied pipers all the

HOW TO STOP SMOKING

way into the sometimes farcical ramifications of this speculative idea . . . but it's difficult to deny that there's some basis in observable fact.

Watch certain men relishing much more than the mere smoke of their large cigar, how they finger and fondle it, lick their wet lips, often greedily, and then wrap their whole mouth over the warm softness, and pucker and draw and suckle and fill themselves, and close their eyes in bliss, lingering, prolonging the moist pleasure . . .

Sometimes they even fall into a little curled sleep . . . and look like babies, soft and fat and innocent and contented for a few lulling moments in their lost Eden. . . .

Is that how you smoke? Are they the satisfactions you are searching for? Are these your remembrances of things past?

Nothing wrong with such satisfactions . . . but you don't have to smoke to get them: nothing to be ashamed about in such lovely memories . . . though why confuse them with the need for a cigarette when you can live them again any time you like in the arms of a lover?

Yet once you understand just how deep-rooted such memories are, how comforting, how necessary, then you'll also begin to realise the pattern you'll be changing . . . and how to change it.

*   *   *

Again, ask yourself: Do you smoke for pleasure? For company? Because you haven't got the courage not to smoke? Or because you think you can't stop?

Many smokers readily admit that most cigarettes are 'negative pleasures' at best, a coughing nuisance at worst: they get some relief from satisfying the craving, and they'd be miserable if they didn't.

'I smoke to stop worrying about smoking.'

But if your smoking is only just for pleasure, if it gives you the occasional 'lift' when you're a bit low, if you merely smoke to be sociable . . . well, you'll have little bother in stopping: you can easily find many more satisfying pleasures without any of the risks, be given a 'lift' by the stimulation of a friendly hug

USING THE MIND TO STOP

or a loving kiss, and enjoy the society of the world and his wife without having to bribe or be bribed by anything so cheap and dangerous as a cigarette.

For you don't have to smoke to be a good companion, you can make a much more valuable gesture of friendship than the offer of a whole box of the most expensive cigars by merely listening to somebody else's troubles for twenty minutes.

As for the courage not to smoke . . .

Do you really fear your friends more than emphysema? Your mates more than the chances of a heart attack? Your colleagues more than cancer?

What sort of friends are they, anyway, that you have to risk serious illness to please them? Who needs mates like that? And if your colleagues are selfish enough to want to see you in the next hospital bed to them when your time comes . . . well, you'd better think about changing jobs — you'll live longer.

But if you think you can't stop, then you must ask yourself: why? What sort of a person are you to remain helpless in the grip of such a deadly and unpleasant habit? Are you an addict?

Few people like to admit, least of all to themselves, that they are anything so 'weak-willed' as that . . . so be sure it's the truth you're telling, and not some track from your oldest long-playing record. Avoid self-pity, don't whinge, face the brutal truth: you're an addict.

And be comforted by the thought that there are worse addicts than you now walking tall and free through the golden landscape: all you're hooked on is nicotine — they've been neck-deep in the hard stuff, up to here, there and back and round the bend . . . mainlining and screaming, weeping, gibbering, crawling . . .

They had to kick it . . .

By comparison all you've got to do is give it a gentle nudge.

'It is quite a three-pipe problem,'
said Sherlock . . .

Don't ever make the mistake of believing that you can't possibly cope with a problem unless you smoke.

True, a cigarette does have a calming effect on some people, just as it can stimulate others — but you smoke it in five minutes, and the effects don't last long. Eventually, you need to smoke more and more for less and less.

Even a chess problem can last for hours.

And a serious problem won't go away because you smoke, and you aren't very likely to think of any truly creative or constructive solution with a headache. So why not learn to live with your human problems? The rest of us do. Everybody's got them, and they're smaller and easier to manage without a temporary smoke-screen.

* * *

And this sort of simple self-knowledge might well be all you need to stop. For you may be starting to see yourself as having surrendered some of your integrity, your freedom . . . and to imagine the sense of self-control you'll have when you've stopped is in itself a great incentive to stopping.

'Know thyself,' said Socrates . . . and your self-knowledge will change the self.

The man who smoked a paper handkerchief

There's a well-known true story which illustrates the power of this self-knowledge.

A man was driving home late one night, fumbled for another cigarette, and realised he'd smoked the last one. In some slight unease, but not yet worried, he stopped the car, and searched for so much as one stub in the little sliding tray under the dash . . . but knowing it was useless, because he was a tidy man so far as his car was concerned, and, yes, it was empty — he always flipped stubs out of the window . . .

He went through his pockets. Nothing.

Not even any loose shreds.

By now he was a bit hot and bothered . . .

Until the thought of loose shreds reminded him that, perhaps, there might just be a few in the corners of the empty packet . . .

USING THE MIND TO STOP

There were, thank God!

Several, at the bottom . . . in the crumpled silver paper as well, vital shreds of most precious tobacco, just about enough to roll a miniature cigarette with a strip of a paper handkerchief, tiny, thinner than a match, more paper than tobacco . . . but a smoke . . . a wisp of saving smoke . . .

And, in his by now almost desperate craving, he tried to light it . . . fingers actually trembling . . . managed to . . .

He suddenly realised what he was doing: there he was, an educated and successful man, teacher of literature, lover of art and music, loving husband and devoted father, a cultured and caring human being . . . sucking at the acrid smoke of a paper handkerchief . . .

Which burnt his lip.

He started the car, and drove home.

He'd stopped smoking.

*   *   *

Yes, you may have smoked for years, been passive, allowed it all to happen . . . but you can change, you've still got time.

Agreed, it sounds too simple to be true.

*   *   *

Stop blaming yourself, and certainly stop blaming other people: parents, pastors, teachers, friends — they can't live for you.

Why drain away useful emotions?

All that matters is that you are currently smoking, that you can stop if you want to, that you can be helped to stop . . . and that you'll soon be starting to stop.

Don't settle for third best.

Demand more from yourself . . . and get it.

You have the right to make mistakes.

You made one when you started smoking — but you don't have to feel guilty about it.

Because now you're going to do something about correcting more than that one mistake.

Take charge of yourself: join the living.

Deciding to decide

Words?

Patronising? Even insulting?

Then ask yourself the obvious question: why?

If none of it's true, so what?

But if it 'speaks to your condition', gets to you — then don't waste those useful emotions: direct them into the process of change, don't swim against your own stream . . . decide . . .

Even the mere act of decision is also important.

Make a formal contract with yourself.

Yes, you're already interested enough in stopping to get this far. You've been thinking about it, perhaps wondering just what sort of smoker you are . . . why you smoke at all, what you actually get out of it. . . .

Take the next small step.

Give it a go: choose to stop smoking.

No, you don't have to stop here and now . . . though who's actually stopping you?

All you have to do is tell yourself that you will be doing the stopping on such and such a day: tomorrow, next week, next month.

Today you do the choosing . . . and we'll do the stopping later.

Understand what you are now doing: read the terms, especially the small print where all the disadvantages are tucked away . . . and, yes, you agree.

If you like, you could even draw up a formal 'statement of intent', and sign it, perhaps with a witness. Might be a bit too threatening, though . . . and too guilt-inducing if you fail the first or second time. But as a light-hearted bit of fun with your wife or husband or lover or friend it would certainly reinforce your decision.

Your pride is now on the bottom line.

Which means that you won't have far to fall.

5

Some of the Means of Stopping

The other main ways of stopping are practical and external: techniques and changes on the outside rather than change from within . . . not so much mere theoretical considerations as means and methods and even gimmicks.

Yes, you have discovered all manner of good reasons to stop smoking, you are (perhaps) persuaded . . . but for you the simple reasons are not enough: to be persuaded is not to be able.

True, everybody needs a motive for stopping . . . but you need more help: a gadget, a method . . . something to hang on to . . .

For you, there are a large number of commercially available products, procedures to follow, places to go.

But you must remember that there's no 'magical' cure that will work the oracle for one and all, once and for all, and that what works for Tom will not necessarily work for Dick — let alone Harry or Aunt Mary.

Mind you, because the need to smoke is often psychological, the most surprising gimmick might just work. Indeed, there's the story about the man who was persuaded that the smell of mothballs was the answer: all he had to do was keep a couple in his old cigarette pocket, sniff at them when tempted, and he'd stop.

And he did stop.

Was never bothered by moths, either.

Keep on taking the tablets

There are various brands of tablets, usually based on an alkaloid substance, lobeline hydrochloride, the purpose of which is to give you a temporary aversion to the taste or smell of tobacco. You take them first thing in the morning, and if you then light a cigarette or inhale anybody else's smoke you'll feel as though you want to be sick. The effects last for up to four or five hours, and you have to keep on taking the dose. Exceed it, and it'll be as though you'd swallowed a mild emetic, and you'll probably be a bit sick.

There are also mouthwashes which work on the same principle. They're usually a weak solution of silver nitrate flavoured with essence of aniseed, which fills the mouth with a foul taste if you inhale smoke, and are also supposed to nullify your craving. You must be extremely careful not to swallow any of these washes, as they are nearly as poisonous as nicotine itself.

Then there are injections, also based on a mixture of lobeline, plus nicotine, which can only be given under medical supervision, and which produce feelings of nausea. One injection in the morning, and you're put off smoking for the rest of the day. Your body just can't take any more nicotine. Force yourself to smoke, and you'd be sick, perhaps even ill. Unfortunately, such injections merely oblige you to stop smoking while they last — they don't do much to reduce the craving for a cigarette. Stop the course of injections, which in any case can only be maintained for about ten days to a fortnight — longer, and there are dangerous side-effects . . . but stop the injections, and you start smoking again.

Anyway, these unpleasant experiences, from tablets to injections, are intended to inhibit your desire for a cigarette, and they often succeed. The trouble is that the effect isn't permanent: stop the treatment, and, unless you have also changed your habits, you'll probably be back where you started . . . having been sicker than even a heavy smoker ever needs to be.

Except during the last few weeks and months of life.

Going through the motions

You can also buy dummy cigarettes of cardboard or plastic, which look and feel more or less like the real thing, depending on how vivid an imagination you've got — though I've seen one with simulated ash and quite a realistic glow at the 'burning' tip . . . though that was in a shop for professional magicians, being the sort they use when they 'produce' lighted cigarettes from glasses of water. Anyway, the commercial variety contain mint-flavoured crystals or methol, and are supposed to enable the 'smoker' to enjoy the illusion of smoking without the smoke — even to 'take away the craving' . . . all of which is what's known as 'going through the motions'.

Some smoker's have said that you'd get the same effect sucking the end of a pen or pencil (though be careful of that graphite), and others have pointed out that it's the smoke they need, not the look or the feel of a cigarette.

'Pretending to smoke is a game for children,' said one. 'And which would you rather have? A good hot dinner or a picture of steak and chips?'

Mixed green salad

Or you could try herbal tobacco for use in handrolled cigarettes: dried lettuce, burdock, dandelion, comfrey, mint, fennel, rosemary . . . almost anything, either alone or in all manner of mixtures. Some are claimed to have that 'genuine Virginia taste', and others to be the 'equivalent of a fine Balkan blend'.

True, they don't contain any nicotine, but undoubtedly produce tars and carbon monoxide, with all of their associated risks . . . so are no real improvement on low-tar cigarettes.

But, again, many smokers have said that while they're smoking at all it might just as well be the real stuff. 'When we were prisoners in Germany during the war,' I was told, 'some of us smoked dried tea-leaves rolled in strips of lavatory-paper — so what's the difference between that and dried cabbage-leaves?'

Though I've also known several contented smokers of such herbal substitutes — two of the other snags being that they are not widely available, and are often difficult to keep alight . . .

'Can't call it smoking, as I spend half me time with matches.'

* * *

During the lung cancer scare of the 1970s the tobacco companies experimented with synthetic cellulose material to provide 'new smoking products' or nicotine-free cigarettes, and were talking about 'reconstituted tobacco' and 'non-volatile additives'. It was suggested at the time that they might as well use 'shredded copies of the London telephone directory'. However, these 'safe' cigarettes were eventually 'produced on a commercial scale', in twenty or more brands . . . but they never caught on.

If you smoke for the drug, and there's no drug, why smoke?

Chewing your way to freedom

There are various nicotine chewing-gums, the best-known being *Nicorette*. The idea is that it's the lack of nicotine which makes you tense or light-headed when you stop smoking . . . so if you can 'taper off slowly' you'll have more chance of controlling these almost inevitable effects. 'Proper use of the gum,' say the manufacturers, 'lessens the withdrawal symptoms, thus enabling you to concentrate on tackling the social and psychological problems of giving up.' Which is a clear enough statement about the nature of the difficulty in stopping: it's not only the chemical dependence on the drug, but the pattern of habits surrounding the smoking.

You chew the gum whenever you feel the urge to smoke, one chew every two seconds for ten chews, then 'rest' the gum under your lip for a minute, then ten more chews, another minute under your lip, ten more chews . . . and so on for thirty minutes. This 'correct rate' of chewing, which you 'train' yourself to achieve with your 'first ten pieces of gum', will 'release the nicotine slowly enough for it to be absorbed through the lining of your mouth'. If you chew 'too quickly',

SOME OF THE MEANS OF STOPPING

or 'swallow saliva too often', you'll get 'hiccups and may experience effects similar to those of smoking too much too quickly'. These include 'irritation of the throat, light-headedness, and nausea'.

You go on chewing ten or more pieces a day for three months, by which time you can 'cut down on the number', with the 'aim of stopping altogether within another month or so'. Though it 'may be a good idea to keep a small supply with you for emergencies'.

It has to be prescribed by a GP, and isn't on the National Health Service list of 'free' prescriptions — so you have to pay the full price, about the same as for cigarettes.

Some people say it works, others that it doesn't . . . and that it's no substitute for the 'real' thing.

And Miriam Stoppard states that 'some research has shown that chewing ordinary gum can be almost as helpful . . .'

On the other hand, Dr Ray Hodgson states that 'several studies indicate that it reduces tobacco consumption more efficiently than a placebo gum not containing nicotine', and goes on to suggest that it's 'most helpful in the initial physiological withdrawal phases of giving up'.

So, if it works for you, why spurn help?

Though remember that it's a help, not a cure: *you* have to do the choosing and the using.

Nothing can do the stopping *for* you.

*   *   *

Another oral method uses various tablets or capsules containing a nicotine substitute, again usually based on lobeline. These are supposed to 'tide you over' any withdrawal symptoms — the claim being that 'lobeline gives the satisfaction of nicotine without the harmful side-effects'.

In conjunction with the sort of programme for stopping to be described later, these substitutes might well be useful — except that there's always the danger that the substitute could itself become indispensable. A crutch remains a crutch no matter what you prefer to call it.

And users have reported that the results are not at all the same as those from nicotine: 'It's the cigarette and the smoke you want,' said one man, 'not just the buzzing in your ears.'

Again, 'studies have shown' that these drugs 'have little effect', and are 'probably not worth using'.

Research

A few years ago there were experiments at a London Addiction Research Unit with 'aerosol inhalers containing nicotine as a short-term substitute' for heavy smokers, based on the principle that nicotine 'taken by mouth is broken down in the liver' and 'never reaches the brain' to give the effect that smokers are wanting. Whereas this 'inhaled nicotine' would be 'absorbed into the bloodstream' and 'carried directly to the brain'.

But these were experiments designed to help 'patients with chronic bronchitis', where 'stopping was crucial to their health' . . . and it's obviously too radical a remedy for stopping while in full possession of your own capacity for succeeding in a programme of self-help.

There are several reports that researchers are working on all manner of other clinical methods to stop smoking.

• For example, Dr Richard Mackarness, of an Alcohol and Drugs Dependency Service in Australia, is enthusiastic about an elegantly simple technique he is currently developing. In this the craving for tobacco is controlled by 'giving a very tiny' and 'precisely measured micro-dose of tobacco extract by injection or drops under the tongue'. He likens it to a 'kind of hair-of-the-dog treatment', which is based on a standard technique for dealing with allergies.

The idea is that 'addiction to cigarettes is evidence of allergy to tobacco smoke'. First, your skin is tested to find the 'minimum strength of tobacco extract' which will 'turn off' your craving. Then, every time you crave for a cigarette, you put a drop of this highly diluted solution under your tongue. 'Within a minute' the craving is gone, and, 'after using the

SOME OF THE MEANS OF STOPPING

drops for a week or two', smoking becomes 'distasteful and the addiction is broken.'

However, Dr Mackarness admits that 'no one yet knows how it works', and that to abolish the craving is 'only part of the battle'. You are still 'left with the psychological elements in the habit or addiction', which will have to be dealt with to 'ensure that the turn-off drops' are used until smoking has lost its appeal.

Your GP will be able to tell you about the possible availability of the Sublingual Drops in this country.

- And finally in this necessarily brief account of research and new development there's the work of Celia and Brian Wright.

They're psychologists who specialise in habit changing, and who run a highly successful clinic in Sussex. Both were once heavy smokers. 'Like a chimney,' says Celia Wright. 'Now I look at someone smoking, and wonder what possessed me.'

They make use of the new information about nutrition, especially about its effect on addiction. For example, vitamin C can be used to help withdrawal from opiate pain-killers and tranquillisers. So, because the pattern of addiction to tobacco is similar, the Wrights believe that vitamin C is indicated to help withdrawal from tobacco.

'The B complex vitamins are important as well,' they state. You need a strong B complex to 'make sure that your nervous system is well nourished' during the process of withdrawal from tobacco, and that you 'have plenty of energy to work with'. Which seems sensible enough, as it's not much use trying to stop smoking if you feel like six inches of chewed string.

They also point out that 'merely by changing the balance between your various foods you can affect your craving'. This principle was established by American researchers who found that smokers tend to smoke more when their urine is acidic. 'By giving them a drug which alkalised their urine' it was possible to reduce their craving by an astonishing 'ninety-five per cent'.

Which means that you can increase the alkalinity of your

blood and urine by changing what you eat. 'Meat, fish, cheese, eggs, and grains,' for example, 'are all acid-forming' . . . whereas 'fresh fruit and vegetables', on the other hand, 'produce an alkaline effect'. Other foods, such as milk, are neutral.

Incidentally, you don't have to give up meat and fish entirely, but merely eat less of them — and munch through as many fresh fruits and vegetables as you can. The bonus being that these alkaline foods are also precisely those which will *keep* you healthy.

'To complete your diet,' state the Wrights, 'you need a good multi-mineral — which will offset the acidity of vitamin C.'

All you have to do is consult your GP, and he will advise you about your own special needs for such vitamins, multi-minerals, and trace elements.

● One day there will undoubtedly emerge a simple and effective course of treatment . . . or, much less likely, tobacco will no longer be grown and manufactured into cigarettes — when your own problems will be solved for you.

But you don't have to wait for that future day.

*   *   *

Finally in this assortment of devices and treatments, there are various filters which are claimed to remove some of the 'harmful tar content from each cigarette smoked'.

● One of these filters looks like an ordinary cigarette-holder, except that it's made from a 'non-toxic transparent plastic' which enables you to see the tar which it traps in a small sump . . . and the sight 'acts as a constant warning'. However, this particular filter is only claimed to remove less than half of the tars — so to use it would merely cut your consumption, for which you'd continue to pay the full price. If you can survive on half the tars, why not smoke half the number of cigarettes?

And if you can cut the number by half, you can stop completely.

● Another such filter comes with a pack of progressively stronger 'strainers'. You use the first for a fortnight, and it

SOME OF THE MEANS OF STOPPING

removes about twenty-five per cent of the tars and nicotine. Then you replace it with one which removes thirty per cent . . . and so on, up to about ninety per cent — by which time you should be 'weaned' off cigarettes. Even if it doesn't work in helping you to stop smoking, you'll at least be reducing your intake of the wrong things . . . though still paying the full price.

* * *

We now come to places, where people with various skills can help you to stop.

Yes, you can stop on your own . . . but people need people, and smokers need people more than most.

Besides, it's so much more enjoyable to stop in good company.

Though three is often a crowd.

A week in the country

There are many Health Farms all over the country: places which specialise in various forms of therapy for most of the common ailments of the twentieth century.

They're usually residential, and you can stay for as briefly as an intensive weekend to as long as a leisurely month, and be dieted, exercised, massaged, bathed, pampered, and relaxed . . . and thus be made fitter, toned up, reduced in weight, and restored to better health. Many now cater for smokers wanting to stop, and a week's course is often enough. Addresses in nearly all health and vegetarian magazines.

Surroundings are always beautiful and restful, the company of others will be a bonus, and even the mere holiday will do you good.

Unfortunately, they tend to be expensive.

Though hardly as expensive as smoking.

And certainly less dangerous . . . though beware of enthusiasts trying to convert you to a diet of carrot juice.

Clinics

Five-day smoking clinics were first devised and run by the Seventh-Day Adventist Church as a 'community service' in this country, and they have been widely adopted by other concerned groups. Fifty or more Local Authorities used to run them, but recent shortage of money has closed many of these.

They are still held in various parts of Britain on a regular basis, and consist of five afternoon or evening sessions of group therapy in some convenient room or hall. Doctors, dieticians, psychologists, and ex-smokers combine to examine the problems of stopping from their different points of view, explain the causes and nature of addiction, describe the results and consequences with slides and films and medical specimens, and then discuss individual cases 'at a personal level in complete confidence' — it being this personal touch and lack of moralising which so many smokers find more useful than all the information.

Another function of these clinics is the 'pairing', which was learned from Alcoholics Anonymous. Two compatible people are introduced and made 'responsible' for each other, and they arrange to keep in contact while they are giving up. They phone several times a day, especially at 'critical' moments, to encourage and receive encouragement and act as a conscience, or they meet for a meal or an evening out . . . and thus help each other to persist.

'A trouble shared is a trouble halved.'

Which in itself is an excellent idea, whether you attend a clinic or not: to have a friend or a lover whom you can phone or meet if you ever need a hand to hold or a shoulder to cry on. It's a sort of Samaritans for smokers.

The claimed rate of success at Seventh-Day Adventist clinics is often high: between seventy and one hundred per cent of those who complete the five-day course.

On the other hand, similar clinics run by Local Authorities have reported that eighty per cent of their smokers who have stopped have 'started again after a year or eighteen months'.

However, most of those who attend are 'probably heavy and long-term smokers who have tried everything else', the clinic being their 'last chance', so even a one-in-five success is fair enough for that one-fifth.

But what about those four out of five?

Anyway, not everybody lives within easy reach of these larger group-therapy sessions . . . and unless you are a Christian you will hardly be very influenced by suggestions that the 'most powerful means' of 'fighting tobacco's stranglehold' is to pray. This is not to question the power of prayer for believers — though I know several priests and monks, even a Jesuit, who'd like to stop but can't . . . yet it ought not to be necessary for a smoker to be a believer in the Christian God before being able to stop.

A more general criticism is that these clinics tend to treat all sorts and conditions of smokers in the same way — whereas the reasons for smoking are varied and complex: not everything works for everybody.

And it must also be remembered that as they tend to attract those heavy smokers who 'have tried everything else', and so are most likely to fail, their company and continued failure often discourages those who have much less difficult problems.

However, if the idea appeals to you, get in touch with your local Health Education Officer or Community Health Council (their numbers will be in the telephone book), and find out if there's a clinic in your area.

Where two or three are gathered together

People deciding to stop smoking, perhaps for the first time, and who form their own groups to give one another moral support, might well succeed. (Incidentally, women tend to find these groups more helpful than men.) The sessions need only be on a fairly casual basis, and don't have to be led by a trained counsellor — because the simple human fact of getting together and talking about their problems could easily provide sufficient incentive to individual members of the group to persevere.

Again, your local Health Education Officer ought to know if and where there are any.

In the United States of America they're called 'Benevolent Pressure Groups', and, in the analogy of the Weight-Watchers, there are even 'Smoke-Watchers' . . . but the British tend to be far less 'structured' with each other, and the idea never really caught on over here.

* * *

However, there is one simple and effective technique which derives from the experience of these American groups. In the jargon of psycho-babble it's called 'role-playing'.

As we have seen, incentive and motivation for stopping are all-important, and so the members of such a group 'induce motivation' by playing various roles in little improvised dramas.

Put yourself in the part of the doctor who has to break the bad news about lung cancer to a smoker.

How do you feel? Sad at the tragedy? Indignant at the waste of a life cut off in its prime? Angry at the stupidity?

Or put yourself in the part of the smoker: it can't possibly be happening to you? You're too young to die? Have you got the courage to face the inevitable pain and death?

Get emotionally involved . . . and you'll begin to realise what you are actually doing to yourself and your family by smoking.

Which will help you and the group to stop thinking about it all as a 'problem' to be 'solved', and to start doing something real and practical about stopping: to start feeling rather than acting.

To say the words 'I have got lung cancer' will force you to face the brutal fact of its possibility: to ask the 'doctor' the stark question 'How long have I got left?' will compel you to ask yourself the same question . . . and ought to provide all the motivation you'll ever need.

How you stop then becomes of little importance.

Of course, you may not fancy joining any such group . . . but, as you'll see later, even two people working together can be just as effective and certainly more enjoyable.

Aversion therapy

Electric-shock 'treatment', associated with lighting up and inhaling, can produce revulsion in even the heaviest smokers. Such aversion therapy is obviously a powerful suppression device, but more experience is needed before it can ensure permanent abstinence. At present its use is limited to small groups of well-motivated smokers acting as guinea-pigs in the three or four research centres at work on the project.

There are also similar experiments to test the possibilities of what's called 'covert sensitisation', in which the smoker is encouraged to relax and enjoy the pleasurable sensations of smoking in comfortable surroundings . . . and is then suddenly shocked with some of the hard and brutal facts about the long-term effects of smoking. Which only reminds me of Pavlov and the conditioned reflexes of his unfortunate dogs.

Smoking yourself sick

Another radical technique, which is undoubtedly effective, but much too dangerous to even consider except under strict medical supervision, is Satiation Smoking . . . or, to put it crudely, smoking yourself sick — getting as close to an earlier death as is necessary to put you off smoking for life.

It's usually carried out in a group, with a doctor or trained therapist present, and your smoking is pushed almost to your outer limits: because you are directed to light up and start puffing, and to keep on puffing every few seconds, cigarette after cigarette . . . until you find yourself loathing every puff. You'll sweat, your heart will race, your head ache and fill with throbbing drums, and you'll want to vomit . . . and probably will. And all the time you'll be reminded of all the reasons for stopping . . . not only then and there and the sooner the better, but for good.

But, obviously, it's extremely dangerous. Please don't ever try it on your own — there *must* be a doctor or therapist present.

Yet all you're doing by smoking like that is accelerating the process: achieving in a short time what smoking will do to you in a longer time — rather like a speeded-up film.

It's not the satiation, but the smoking.

Even the very thought works with some squeamish people.

A modified form of this technique, which you can use with no more danger than that caused by ordinary smoking, is to concentrate on the negative aspects of each cigarette: allow the smoke to curl up around your eyes and make them smart, keep it in your mouth until it burns your tongue and throat, inhale it deeper, hold it in your lungs for longer . . . if it makes you cough, so much the better.

Then ask: 'Why am I doing this? Where's the pleasure?'

And the unpleasant memories will come in useful in the process of stopping.

Under the 'fluence'

Hypnosis sounds rather dramatic, and summons up an easy dream of being soothed into a deep trance by a man with luminous eyes, and told that you will never smoke again . . .

There's a click of fingers, you wake up . . . and that's that: you never smoke again.

In fact, hypnotherapy is usually only a minor part of a more general treatment, used as an aid to relaxation. You have to be referred to a registered hypnotist by your GP, and it's no good at all if you are one of the seventy to eighty per cent of those who don't respond to it.

Again, 'studies have shown' that the evidence is 'incomplete and that no clear conclusions could be drawn about the usefulness of hypnosis' in the 'treatment' of smoking.

SOME OF THE MEANS OF STOPPING

And remember that nobody 'under the fluence' can be made to do anything which they'd refuse to do in ordinary life. So you most certainly won't stop smoking when asleep if you don't want to stop while you're wide-awake.

Going on the needles

There are also the various options available through 'alternative' medicine, ranging from the by now 'respectable' homoeopathy to the newer acupuncture. All are highly specialised, and you'll need to enquire in your own area.

But, for example, acupuncturists claim to 'cure' smoking by inserting fine needles into various parts of the body — and I've been told that some use the lobe of your left or right ear. The needles are screwed into tiny metal studs, rather like pinheads, and every time you want a cigarette you simply touch or tap one of them, a 'message' is transmitted to the appropriate centre of the brain, and you can resist the craving.

The claimed rate of success is supposed to be as high as seventy per cent, but there's no real way of knowing for sure. I've only known of a few people who've tried it . . . and the treatment worked for those with the faith.

Remember the man and the mothballs?

If a method works for you — then that's it, thank you very much.

'But,' says Charles Bentley, a successful acupuncturist, 'beware of people who promise to "cure" you of smoking by sticking pins in your ears or wherever. The trained practitioner will insist upon a thorough investigation and remedial treatment of the underlying imbalance of need which causes smoking — and only then would provide a safe and effective treatment for the basic tensions which are a part of our twentieth-century environment.'

Which is another way of saying that smoking is merely a symptom of something else: find out what, understand *why* you smoke . . . and then you can start stopping.

And if a trained acupuncturist can help you in that way . . . well, why not?

Daily routine orders

Then, for people who feel happier being told what to do and when to do it, who prefer to know where they stand and where they are allowed to sit down, how far they can move and in which direction . . . for them there's the technique of the List, the Set of Rules and Regulations Governing the Prohibition of Smoking.

The fact that they draw up their own Regulations and make their own Rules is irrelevant: all they need to do is keep them. True, some may prefer to be told by somebody else, made to toe the lines laid down, walk the straight and narrow . . . and would find it even easier to obey a partner than themselves. Which could be fun for both of them: for some of us are Nature's sergeants, and some of us will never rise from the ranks.

But if you enjoy a structured life, if people adjust their clocks by your comings and goings, if you know where you will be at three o'clock next Saturday afternoon, and have got a typewritten list of 'Contents' stuck on the back of the medicine-cabinet door . . . then try issuing yourself some Daily Routine Orders.

Start with one: you will never smoke in bed.

When you've obeyed it long enough to know that it's as much a part of your world as the hourly time-signal on your digital fifteen-function wristwatch, add two more: You will never smoke in the loo . . . You will never smoke when walking . . .

When these have established themselves, add three more: never before breakfast . . . never after supper . . . never when driving . . .

Then you start on the individual cigarettes themselves: count to five before you ever open the packet . . . then to ten . . . then to twenty . . . twenty-five . . .

SOME OF THE MEANS OF STOPPING

Count before you actually light it . . .

Never immediately after breakfast . . . never immediately before supper . . . never during any meal . . .

And so on, until, eventually, you have covered every hour and circumstance and cigarette of your day and night . . .

You've stopped.

But if you're that good at obeying Rules, why not Issue the Ultimate Instruction now?

Stop!

6

Stopping on Your Own

We now come to the simplest and easiest way for the ordinary smoker to stop smoking without very much external help . . . and to stay stopped.

It's going to be an extremely important change in your habits and behaviour, so you'll need to think, to prepare, to plan.

You'd hardly enter for the London Marathon without at least trotting a few miles round the block to see how you'd last the course. Why should this course of action be any different?

You'll need to think about what you're intending to do, how best to prepare for stopping, what plans to make against possible failure. The thinking may have taken you years, and you might still have a lot to do. The necessary preparations we'll deal with when you need to start making them. And we'll postpone all thoughts about failure at least until you've stopped.

Nicotine and habit

So, what keeps you a smoker?

There are two main strands in the cable that attaches you to smoking: chemical dependence, and social habit.

Chemical dependence (or addiction, if you want the loaded word) is caused by the use of a drug (in this case nicotine), which so acts on the brain and body that you believe you can't do without it. To understand this fact is to recognise that it's going to be harder to stop than it was to start.

Social habit?

If you've smoked forty a day you have performed a satisfying little ritual every twenty minutes or so of your waking life: opening the packet that has been designed by experts to be a pleasurable artefact to see and handle, and certainly easy to open . . . or perhaps it's your expensive cigarette case, gold or silver or chrome or leather, so beautiful and efficient . . . then sliding out the cigarette, enjoying the smell and the look and the feel of it, smooth and delicate, tapping the end on the nearest surface . . . then lighting up with a match or a lighter, each with their own mystique, the cradling of the flame in the hands, or the flick of power, with boxes and lighters being like small toys, especially lighters, lovely things to finger and touch and dicker with . . . and then all the personal mannerisms of smoking, how you hold and play with the cigarette, how you inhale, how you hold the smoke in your lungs, how you let out those pale blue clouds and columns and lingerings, gentle or masterfully, through flared nostrils or in controlled rings . . . what you do with the ash . . .

Have you ever noticed how many ways there are of doing something interesting with the ash? From the full ceremonial tap after every puff to the complicated series of little flicks between puffs . . . all the way to the fastidious delicacy required to maintain its virginal fragility for as long as possible before it droops and drops . . . feathering . . .

All again and again and again, time after time, hour after day after week after month after year after year . . .

With the whole ritual even more intricate and engrossing if you roll your own or smoke a pipe.

So, by these thousands and thousands of repeated actions, you have laid down a gratifying pattern, which is as much a part of your life and personality as the way you eat chips or drink tea or comb your hair.

You may even find yourself with a cigarette in your mouth, and not actually remember lighting it.

Smoking has become a reflex.

One at a time

Each cigarette is a habit in itself, so anything you can do to interfere with the pattern of each one will help you change the larger pattern.

'Keep a rubber-band round the packet,' says Miriam Stoppard, 'so that you are aware of opening it.'

Or, during your week or month of preparation for stopping, you could keep an accurate record of each cigarette you smoke. Don't make a Big Production of it: you're not writing a Journal to pass on to your children's children. Have a piece of paper tucked into the packet, and, before you light up, note the time, and why you think you're going to smoke this next one.

'Eleven, morning coffee, always have one with it.'

Will take, say, fifteen seconds, and it will be useful in your self-discovery of your pattern of smoking . . . but those few seconds will slow you down just that little bit, will break the habit of that cigarette. Don't light it until you've made the note. Yes, it's a nuisance — but it's meant to be.

A week should convince you that smoking is as much habit as addiction . . . though it's unlike most other habits.

There's no chemical dependence in biting your nails, putting on your tie before you've pulled on your trousers, or always folding your bus ticket in quite that intricate way. And what physical harm does it do to count the paving stones between here and the next lamppost?

Kicking the stuff

To remove a chemical dependence is obviously much harder than merely changing a habit.

As we have seen, most smokers claim that they could 'give it up any time, no bother'.

If they know all about the long-term effects of smoking, and still enjoy it, still choose to smoke — that's their decision.

True, it sounds as though they have a low opinion of their own worth: 'What does it matter if I *do* get lung cancer? Who cares whether I live or die?'

But if they've thought about stopping, tried — and failed . . . what's gone wrong? Where's the bother?

And the answer, as we have also seen, is brutal: whether they care to admit it or not, they're hooked.

And in trying to give it up they haven't used a comprehensive strategy, one based on simple physical and psychological principles.

Good intentions are not enough.

It's not much use trying to stop on impulse.

To succeed, you must make a conscious effort, you've got to change the priorities of your life . . . and work at changing over days and weeks, perhaps even a couple of months.

It's taken you a long time to hone your habits to perfection, so a week or two of structural alterations will be needed to establish a new set . . . and you can't just turn off an addiction like a tap: you've got to flush out the tanks and pipes.

* * *

Resolving to stop is easy enough . . .

'Give up smoking?' said Mark Twain. 'There's nothing to it! I've done it at least twenty-five times!'

To stick at it is more difficult — unless you understand what's going on, what's happening to you, why you feel so terrible, why you've got such a splitting headache.

You've got to do *two* things: overcome your chemical dependence on nicotine, and change the pattern of your life.

And you've got to do them at the same time.

Warning!

The first three or four days will be the worst.

More about these withdrawal symptoms later. There's a lot you can do to lessen their effects — and they're rarely as bad as they seem on paper, and needn't last. Though you will almost certainly have a mild headache, which will come and go for a day or two.

But bite on that bullet!

By the end of the week the craving for a smoke will have become much less intense, and may even have gone.

Stick at it for a fortnight, and you've probably kicked it.

Please notice that it's only 'probably' . . . because, for all manner of reasons, you may slip back. Some new stress might tempt you to try the old consolation, over-confidence may take you into those smoke-filled rooms, or somebody could make you an offer you don't think you can refuse . . .

Shock! Horror! You've smoked again!

Yet all you will have done is *slipped*, not fallen.

And even if you do fall flat on your back, and finish the packet, it's always possible to get up, dust off, and start all over from the beginning . . . Yes?

Will power isn't everything

Don't make the common mistake of trying to do it by Will-power.

'Must pull myself together. Get a firm grip. Buckle down. None of the old nonsense. I *will* give up smoking.'

Because you'll get discouraged if you 'give in' or 'lose' the struggle, and probably despise your own weakness.

But it's not a battle you're fighting, it's not arm-wrestling, there's no opponent.

All you are doing is merely changing a habit: it's not a war with 'winners' or 'losers' . . . but a new way of living.

No, rather than make eternal vows you may not be able to keep, the breaking of which will lower your self-esteem, reduce your necessary self-confidence, it's far better to be provisional.

'I *choose* not to smoke. . . .'

Yes, you may still be tempted, may still light one 'last' cigarette, the 'final' pipe . . . but you haven't 'lost,' you're not back at the bottom of the pit. Who's perfect?

'I *choose* not to smoke. . . .'

Even the mere saying of it helps, and simple repetition will encourage a growing resistance to the craving. Because how you think, how you use the power of your mind, has an immediate effect on your body — you not only weaken the craving, but gradually bring your habits under your own control.

You do the choosing!

Think about what you are doing — for whatever our mind accepts as our own image, we tend to become.

We are what our thoughts make us.

It doesn't much matter whether or not you yet believe that you *can* stop smoking, so long as you go on telling yourself that you are *choosing* to stop — because through repetition it will permeate your mind, and predispose you to the confidence you need for success.

'I *choose* not to smoke. . . .'

Believing in yourself

The next step is to acquire a new self-image.

Imagination is a more powerful function than the will. We can always imagine even the apparently impossible: knocking out the Champion of the World in the first round . . . being carried off by that dishy Star of Stage and Screen . . . winning the Pools . . .

No, imagination is hardly ever a problem!

To *imagine* yourself succeeding is the easiest part of the process, the greatest of pleasures . . . and absolutely essential.

See yourself not smoking, your mouth no longer tasting like that damp ashtray, your breath as sweet as bread-and-butter, eyes bright, lungs clear and full of fresh air . . . no longer coughing . . . more money in your pocket . . .

Believe in your own self-image . . . and then *live* as though that belief were already fact.

It soon will be!

Don't worry about whether or not you'll still be a non-smoker tomorrow or next week or next year: it's happening now.

The exercise of will power isn't always some titanic struggle . . . but can merely be the gradual accumulation of many small habits. You build even the biggest house with bricks . . . one at a time.

All you've got to do for a start is see yourself as a non-smoker, and say: 'I choose not to smoke, not now, not for this next minute . . . these next sixty seconds . . . one at a time.'

And at the same time you start changing circumstances . . .

How other people stop

It is possible to stop? Just like that?

You and the Duke of Edinburgh.

So how do other people do it?

- Some can decide in advance when they're going to stop, such and such a date, cut down their consumption gradually, and then stop for good at the end of the process.

But be careful, as it's harder this way than it looks. 'One more or less won't make much difference, will it?' So you have another. And another. And another . . .

There's also the chance that as you smoke less you might start to enjoy each cigarette more — which would induce you to go on.

- Some decide not to smoke while standing or walking or driving, or not before noon or after six o'clock in the evening, not before or after meals, and so on. Then they extend these self-imposed restrictions, and end by smoking only two or three a day . . . by which time it's easy to stop altogether.

But that method requires a very special sort of person to manage.

- Some stop after an attack of tonsillitis, or a bad cold. Seems that such infections tend to inhibit smoking . . . and you could take the chance to stop: the infection does the inhibiting, and you do the stopping. 'There is a tide in the affairs of men . . .'

Again, as we have seen, some people have stopped after seeing the disgusting gobbets of tar-blackened phlegm they've coughed up during a bronchial spasm . . . which is one of the more dramatic ways of being persuaded.

- And some go in for a 'cure' . . . like one of those gargles every morning with the commercial preparation of chemicals which render the taste of a cigarette so foul that to smoke would make them sick.

But if you're strong-minded enough to go on with such an unpleasant daily treatment, you can easily manage to stop smoking without it. And the very preference for a 'cure' reveals that the smoker isn't yet prepared to take full responsibility for stopping. Failure can be blamed on the 'cure', not the smoker.

You can do whatever you want to do

In fact, there are probably as many ways of stopping as there are of losing weight, and there's very little hard evidence that any one is more successful than another. It all depends on how highly motivated you are.

If you want to use the powers of your will and imagination, and take positive action — you can. Almost whatever you then do will work . . . for you.

If you merely think that it might just be a rather good idea to think about it at some time — well, you'll be wasting your time.

It's best in the end to stop from the beginning, best to have a few (perhaps) difficult days and be over with it for good. Why drag it out? Why prolong even the comparatively slight inconvenience?

And, honestly, it'll be easier than you think!

Full dress rehearsal

You can make it even easier by starting to stop before you actually stop, by rehearsing, getting used to the idea.

Decide, say, a month in advance, that on such and such a day you are going to stop, prepare for it, start making all sorts of small changes in your pattern of habits.

• There's no particular virtue in knotted hair-shirts, so pick the easiest time for you to stop.

HOW TO STOP SMOKING

It's no good trying ten minutes before that all-important interview for a new job, or the first few hours of the morning after the night before.

If by your self-questioning you have discovered that you smoke most at work, decide that you'll be lighting your last cigarette as you knock-off on Friday evening — this will give you until Monday morning to change your pattern. Of if you smoke most at home, then decide that you'll be stopping as you leave for work. Or at the beginning of your next holiday. Or illness . . .

In other words, decide to stop at any natural break in your routine . . . and mark the date on every available calendar. Choose a special day, a birthday or anniversary. You'll be happy, and probably under the minimum of stress.

That's the day you'll be working towards.

- Then, having chosen that day for stopping, start changing small things and actions: if you use a lighter, change to matches . . . use your left hand to hold your cigarette, or, if you're left-handed, your right . . . put the cigarette into a different place between your lips, the other side or the middle . . . break the pattern . . .
- Then decide which cigarette of your day is the most necessary or the most enjoyable: the first on waking up? Or the last before turning over to go to sleep at night? The one with your coffee at eleven o'clock? Or the one after tea at four?

This will obviously be the one most difficult to give up . . . and this will be the time when you'll need everything going for you to resist.

So it will be well worth your while to get in a few full-dress rehearsals.

The best smoke of the day

Merely to pick one example, which will have to stand in for all, suppose you've discovered that the cigarette with your morning coffee is the one you enjoy the most.

STOPPING ON YOUR OWN

The particular circumstances in which you drink it will vary with who or what or where you are: from home to work's canteen, office to school staffroom, or that friendly little place around the corner.

Do everything you can to change your routine: have tea instead of coffee, drink it in the lounge or the garden instead of the kitchen, in a different part of the canteen . . . somewhere else than that same fuggy old nattering staffroom . . . or find an entirely new friendly little place around another corner. . . .

Then, instead of merely drinking your tea or glass of milk or fruit juice or whatever, concentrate on enjoying everything about the occasion: the shape of the cup and saucer or glass, the feel, the colour, the warmth or the cold to your fingers, the aroma . . . and even milk has a lovely hint of meadows on its breath . . .

Look around, watch the people, the faces . . .

Take your time about that first sip . . . let the taste fill your mouth . . . what's the hurry?

Then another sip, know it in your mouth and throat, experience the flow, the flavour, the pleasure. Say to yourself: 'This is enough for now without a cigarette. Later on, when I've enjoyed this to the last drop, in the warm glow of remembrance, perhaps in half an hour — well, then I'll have a cigarette.'

And so you'll get used to the whole idea of enjoying things for their own sake, one at a time: living in the continuous present for all you're worth.

No, you're not going to stop smoking now, not yet . . . nor even trying to cut down too much. But merely getting used to the idea, flexing your moral muscles, replacing one little set of habits by a different set of experiences.

Yet stop smoking that one cigarette, and you'll find the others all that much easier to live without.

Smoke is no substitute for life.

Enjoying life for its own sake

Start to separate your experiences.

Don't any longer confuse the varied tastes and textures of bacon and eggs for breakfast with the cigarette afterwards.

Tea is delicious on its own, so many brands and blends . . . why mix them into sameness with tobacco?

Coffee is a whole world of flavour, all those rich aromas . . . how can smoke possibly improve the already perfect?

And why spoil even the cheapest wine? 'Chill before serving,' it says on the label . . . so why burn your tongue before drinking?

You've got to do everything you can to ease and tease out that smoke. It's become part of your life, wreathing and reaching into almost every last hole and corner . . . and nearly everything you do is somehow associated with cigarettes, eating and drinking, working and playing and loving . . . highs and lows, pains and pleasures . . .

So begin now to start the unravelling . . .

Learn how to work without the smoke getting in your eyes, to play without having to interfere with the game.

Enjoy your peaks for their own sake, live with your lows on your own resources.

If you're under the weather, why add clouds of fug to the clouds?

If you're on the top of the mountain, why obscure the view?

Music is enough . . . listen to it with your total attention.

What more does any good book need?

And what can a cigarette do for a kiss except burn your lips and make it taste like a damp ashtray?

All of which is most excellent preparation for that soon-coming day when you'll have stopped, when you'll be on your own . . . and enjoying every minute of pleasure and health.

Change your brand, change your life

Another simple change you can make before stopping is to change your brand of cigarette.

STOPPING ON YOUR OWN

Suppose you've decided to give yourself a full month to prepare.

At the end of the first week change your brand to one with less tar and slightly less nicotine. All tobacconists should have the official list of *Tar and Nicotine Yields* on display. Don't try to go for broke by reducing the nicotine content too much all at once, or you'll probably miss your usual intake, and get irritable.

If you can afford it, buy your whole week's suply in one go. This will start convincing you just how expensive it all is, and also reduce the number of your visits to a tobacconist.

You're never going to smoke your favourite brand again.

Yes, already changing your habits.

Then, at the end of the second week, change the brand yet again: slightly less nicotine . . . perhaps filtered . . .

You'll still be smoking — but, without missing too much to bear, you'll be getting just that little bit less from each cigarette.

And then, finally, at the end of the third week, change the brand for the last time: even less nicotine.

One week's supply.

Never need to go into a tobacconist's shop again.

When you've smoked that lot you're stopping.

* * *

On the last day of your smoking you make quite sure that you understand why you're going to stop.

Yes, it's old ground to go over: health, independence, money, or whatever . . . but it will reinforce your decision.

You also review the ways and means you'll be using to help you stop: the new habits you'll be acquiring, the various procedures for resisting temptation, and so on . . . which will give you confidence in your ability to stop.

The final fling

There's one last reinforcer you can use.

Remember the Satiation Smoking used in Aversion Therapy?

Well, the day before you stop, during the final couple of hours, go in for a session of heavy smoking.

Not if you are over forty, over-weight, diabetic, suffering from high blood pressure or any sort of heart trouble or respiratory disease, and certainly not if you're pregnant.

In any case, it would be a good idea to tell your GP that you are going to stop smoking, and what you are intending to do on this last day — and take his advice.

But, subject to his approval, have a final deliberately unpleasant session.

No tea or coffee or alcohol, just cigarettes.

Smoke two, one after the other . . . not casually, but sticking at it, getting through them with fixed purpose.

Short pause . . .

Then two more . . .

Concentrate on how you're feeling: headache yet?

Another short pause . . .

Then two more . . .

By now you may be having to force yourself, but the least signs of wanting to be sick, or palpitations, or dizziness . . . stop!

But ask yourself: 'Are these the pleasures of smoking?'

Two more cigarettes . . .

Be honest with yourself: admit your symptoms, experience your feelings, store up memories of how terrible it all is. You'll use these memories when you're tempted after you've stopped.

If you possibly can, smoke two more . . . but stop at twelve, or you'll make yourself really ill.

There you go: that's smoking for you!

Accentuate the positive

To change a bad habit, substitute a better one.

Be positive rather than negative.

For example, to stop biting your nails, form the habit of caring for them, cleaning and shaping, and being pleased with the result . . . and *see* yourself with normal nails.

So with smoking: form new habits of non-smoking.

The secret is to set yourself easily-achieved tasks.

Don't try to jump over the mountain in one tremendous leap, but climb up and over one small ridge at a time.

Even a journey of ten thousand miles starts with a single step.

Yes, to stop smoking may now seem a journey twice around the world and back. But to go without the *next* cigarette is that single step. And all you've got to do is go on going without one cigarette . . .

'I choose not to smoke the *next* cigarette. . . .'

The first Friday night in the rest of your life

It's easiest to stop smoking at the beginning of some natural break in your usual pattern of life. You're going to change that pattern, anyway, so you must take every advantage you can.

Going to work is an established pattern with most of us: we get up at the same time every working day, catch the regular bus or train, see the same sights on the same route, the same faces, follow the same old rut . . . all of which reinforces the pattern of our smoking. That first cigarette when we wake up, one after breakfast, one on the bus or train, one when we start work, one over coffee . . . and so on.

So why not start to stop on Friday evening?

The pattern of your week has been broken, you don't have to go to work tomorrow, you'll have all day on Saturday and Sunday: sixty or more hours in which you can change the pattern of dependence.

Better still, why not start at the beginning of the Christmas or Easter holiday? Your annual fortnight or three weeks?

You'll have more time, more chance to establish new ways.

Because it can't be attempted casually, or while you're

concerned with something else: it's a course of semi-medical treatment, self-administered, with elements of amateur psychology, intended to change the most important person you know.

So you'll need to concentrate on yourself, take every possible precaution . . . and take it all seriously.

* * *

Suppose you've decided to start on Friday evening.
- The first thing to do is throw away your cigarettes (that's if you've got any left over from your last week of smoking or your final unpleasant session) and all the necessary bits and pieces: lighter or matches, cigarette case, ashtray . . . the lot.

(Pipe and pouch as well, of course.)

Yes, perhaps there's some expensive gear involved — but you've been puffing money away up in smoke for years, so what's a few more pounds in a better cause?

You *could* give the stuff to a friend — but why do to a friend what you are now no longer going to do to yourself?

No, merely say, 'I choose not to smoke any more of this, I don't need any more of these bits and pieces.' And throw the lot away.

Burn the cigarettes on the fire, or flush them down the loo. That way you can't give in to the inevitable temptation to retrieve them from the rubbish bin at half-past two in the morning.

Burn your bridges and your boats.

Now there's no way back.

Five-finger exercises

Mind you, as you've probably been playing with those things for years, you'll miss them as familiar objects.

So keep your hands busy with a pen or pencil or a trinket. Some people play with a small stone of distinctive shape and variegated colours, or a Japanese carving, a piece of engraved ivory, or an interesting little shell — even worry beads. . . Touch and examine and explore and fiddle with these as your fingers used to with their lighter or a pipe. Or what about treating yourself to an 'executive' toy? You'll be saving money in the long run.

Yes, go on playing with fire

Incidentally, if you enjoy actually lighting cigarettes, and get conscious pleasure from playing with your lighter, flicking it and controlling the flame, there's no need to deny yourself. Get some small (even large) decorative candles, and arrange them about the place, and go on with your enjoyment of lighting and controlling, trimming the wicks, watching the flames.

Just be careful of the slightly increased risk of fire.

But those flickering little jewels can be fascinating . . . and soothing — which will be all to your good.

And as your sense of smell improves you can experiment with perfumed candles, joss sticks . . . incense . . .

Making a clean start

It's also a very good idea to send your clothes to the cleaners — preferably during your last week before stopping. You probably can't smell them, but they're kippered in smoke . . . and as your sense of smell recovers you'll be reminded of tobacco.

Everything in your room (even the whole house) will also be kippered, so give it a thorough airing as well.

Fresh air is going to be your friend.

And invest in a few large tins of throat lozenges — each a different flavour.

And so to bed

Friday evening, and you've thrown away your cigarettes.

Get ready for bed earlier than usual.

Tiredness in its many forms is an enemy of the will.

Because they stay up very late at night, and don't get enough rest and sleep — with merely resting in the bed being almost as important as the sleeping . . . most people stumble up and out in the morning with eyes like burnt rock-cakes. With nerves already jangling for a cigarette, how can they resist?

- First, go for a short brisk walk. Don't wear yourself to a frazzle, it isn't a race — but take plenty of deep breaths, get your heart pumping, blood flowing.
- Come back to a warm bath or shower. Not too hot, as the purpose is relaxation, not endurance. Wash your hair thoroughly, scrub your nails, remove the last traces of smoke. Pamper yourself, use plenty of soap, get really clean, take your time, wallow in the comfort, make friends with your body, enjoy your nakedness. All this will help you to unravel, gentle your nerves, take your mind off of what you think are your troubles.
- If you enjoy a night-cap of warm milk or Ovaltine or drinking chocolate, have a cup — but don't drink tea or coffee or alcohol. You want natural sleep, not too much stimulation or booziness.

(It's also another very good idea to avoid tea and coffee for the first few days, as the slight stimulation may cause your system to wonder where all the nicotine has gone. The fact is that many smokers find it harder to stop because of what they eat and drink. Some foods and condiments are obviously stimulating to the palate — think of pepper and curry, mustard, chilli, vinegar, pickles, horseradish. So avoid pulling the trigger on any craving for a cigarette. When your sense of taste returns, you won't need quite so much Madras Special, anyway.)

- If you usually grope your way out of sleep in the morning, and light a cigarette first thing, put a glass of lemon or orange juice ready by the side of your bed. When you reach for your cigarettes they won't be there — but the juice will be. Drinking it will be that vital 'something to do' — the pattern will be disrupted. And the clean taste will be fresh, and the acidity will help get rid of the nicotine.
- And as you snuggle down into the clean sheets, comfort

yourself with the thought that you've now chosen to stop smoking. Yes, you're a fully responsible human being in charge of your own life . . . and you're worth the effort it's taking.

One thing's for sure: you won't be smoking in your sleep!

Get out of bed on the wrong side

In the morning get up a bit earlier.
Tell yourself that you've chosen to stop smoking . . .
Who needs it?
- Drink that glass of juice at once . . . slowly . . . enjoy . . .
This is the first day in the rest of your life . . . yes?
- Change your routine in every way you can: get out of bed on the other side . . . even slide out of the end . . .
That's a daft thing to do?
Then laugh at yourself!
- Have a bath or shower before breakfast . . . but no wallowing.

When you're dry, have a brisk friction rub all over with a warm coarse towel . . . or you could use those proprietary mittens. But really work at it, get the circulation surging . . . arms, legs, back, belly, buttocks. All of which will get you wide awake, more and more alive . . . without a cigarette!

You've chosen to stop. . . .
- Clean your teeth with a different toothpaste, rinse your mouth thoroughly with warm water . . . and then drink a glass or two.
- You may not fancy it warm at first, but persist. Start with the proverbial thimbleful, and work your way up. It's all part of the essential process of flushing the nicotine out of your system . . . and you ought to feel as though you're sloshing as you move. Warm unsweetened lemon juice will do if you can't bear warm water, or you could try half and half. You'll obviously feel a bit bloated to start with . . . but every visit to the loo is another step to freedom, so enjoy the thought.

* * *

While in the loo, remember that you may just be a bit constipated for a few days: which is nothing to worry about . . . your body is merely adjusting itself to your new pattern of behaviour, and will soon settle into regularity again. So don't take any laxatives. Besides, all the fruit you're going to munch through will help.

New every morning is the dish of fruit

- For breakfast start with some of that fruit; apples, oranges, slices of pineapple, grapes, peaches, nectarines . . . drink plenty of juice — a different one every morning. Enjoy all those sharp or sweet or even sour tastes, textures, bite into the crispness, savour the succulence. Try a small jar of natural yogurt.
- Have a treat you can look forward to from the time you get up: that posh marmalade you can't usually afford . . . French toast or German bread or Swedish rye or go all Danish or Dutch. . . .

Take your time, relax. . . .

- If you usually listen to the news on the radio, switch to music on another station. The news will almost certainly be middling to bad or catastrophic, so give it a rest — then you won't have to worry over things you can do little about. If you usually listen to music, try another sort for a change: Bach for boogie-woogie, or hard rock for a brass band . . . and really listen, pay attention, get all you can from the experience.

This is why you got up a bit earlier.

- If you usually read a newspaper over breakfast, change it for a few weeks, see the world from a new angle . . . or, better still, go without one for a few weeks: what will you be missing? Try a new magazine or a paperback . . . or look through *Radio Times*, and select one programme for the evening. And only one, because you're not going to be spending much time slumped in front of that television. But it will be something more to look forward to, a time in the future, a pleasure to come.

STOPPING ON YOUR OWN

Go on taking your time. . . .

Millions of people are now hurriedly gulping down a snatched cup of tea or coffee, grabbing half a slice of burnt toast. No wonder their nerves are fraught . . . can't wait for a smoke!

Remind yourself that you've chosen to stop smoking. . . .

If you feel that you can't really start the day without something more than fruit, have one or two lightly-boiled eggs as well . . . but don't get stodged . . . stay loose . . .

- When you've finished eating, don't hang about, don't keep sitting at the table: that's when you probably lit a cigarette.

Clean your teeth again. You're beginning to break the connection between the taste of food and the memory of smoke in your mouth.

- Now get dressed, and go out for a brisk walk.

It need only be for five or ten minutes, but breathe deeply, enjoy the day and the weather — even if it's raining.

- Suck one of those throat lozenges — you may not have a sore throat from having stopped, but it will at least give your mouth something to do in replacement for sucking at a cigarette.

Perhaps, if you really can't do without a newspaper, you could walk to the shop for a change instead of having delivery.

It may all sound much too easy to be effective — though why should it be complicated or difficult? But get out into the fresh air as often as possible — especially after every meal. No slumping half-asleep in your favourite chair.

Fresh air isn't smoke . . . and you're ventilating your system.

And the exercise itself is important, because it tunes the body, makes it fitter, enables you to cope with stress . . . and simply helps you to feel better.

Monday, Black Monday

Suppose that you haven't been able to start to stop smoking at the beginning of your annual holiday, or at some other longer break, but have only had the weekend to replace the old pattern.

Well, on Monday morning there you are, on your way to work: the same old bus or train, the same sights, the same faces, the same places, the same long-established routine. . . .

Unless you're careful, that familiar pattern will reassert itself . . . and you'll be gasping for a smoke.

- So try going to work by a different route, even though it takes a bit more time. After all, you've got up earlier. Take the bus instead of the train, or the train instead of the bus. Remember to travel in a *non-smoking* compartment. Read the paper or a book instead of merely looking out of the window without really seeing the passing world, don't let things happen to you, but be actively involved in as much as possible, be interested in everything going on around you. And don't let it be any old book, but that one you've been meaning to read for weeks. Or start talking to the person next to you . . .
- Or get on your bike, and enjoy the ride . . .
- Or walk some or even all of the way . . . some people even run all the way: ever thought of that London Marathon?

But do anything to change your route, the morning, the day . . .

*   *   *

You probably can't do very much about your place of work, but you could perhaps shift or rearrange your desk or bench, put up a different picture, find a different pin-up or pop star or Athena reproduction of a watercolour by Turner or a photograph of your husband or wife or lover . . . or have a bunch of flowers where you can see and smell them.

- If you have to use the telephone a lot, be extra careful — because, as Miriam Stoppard has pointed out, a 'common ritual is automatically lighting a cigarette as soon as it rings, and smoking while answering it'. So move the temptation to another part of your desk — then 'you have to use the opposite hand from usual'. Change your pattern, 'doodle while talking', or 'walk up and down if the flex is long enough' . . . anything to disturb the sequence of movements which used to lead to you reaching for the packet, the lighter . . .

Which is where that Executive toy would come in handy.

Carry on choosing

You must watch for the almost inevitable tensions at work, those pressures which cigarettes are supposed to help you survive.

Letters that must be typed in the next ten minutes, invoices checked by ten o'clock, the next batch of parts machined by eleven, the arithmetic books marked before the next lesson . . . somebody being bitchy, the foreman on his high horse . . . that Big Meeting with a new client . . . stress, complications, the bad patch, the sticky bit . . .

All you need is a quick smoke, and you'll be all right . . . Yes?

Take a deep breath . . .

You've chosen to stop smoking, remember?

Nip off to the loo, rinse your mouth, drink a glass of water or the fruit juices you've brought to work with you.

Come back, and start again. Suck a boiled sweet . . . worry about your teeth later. Try a throat lozenge. Chew gum. Munch an apple, or eat a few mixed nuts.

But don't ever think of any of these delicious things as a mere substitute for a cigarette . . . they are enjoyable additions to your day, pleasures to be enjoyed.

Some people have tried root-ginger at these times. Whenever temptation comes, they put a tiny sliver of the root into their mouth, and the strong tingling flavour seems to satisfy the craving. And after a few weeks they no longer need it. But with others it might just stimulate more than it substitutes . . . so be careful. Gently, gently . . .

HOW TO STOP SMOKING

How to resist temptation

What do you do if a friend or colleague or workmate offers you a cigarette? An offer you don't feel you can refuse?

It's one of those depressing facts of human nature that some smokers may experience genuine guilt at your stopping, and really want to stop themselves . . . but will still try to persuade you to 'have one' with them — perhaps through envy, not liking to see you do what they know they should be doing.

Well, remember that when the Mafia make an offer you can't refuse, you die if you don't accept — but this one's the other way round: you stand a higher risk of dying if you do accept!

'Thanks all the same, but I've chosen to stop.'

This reinforces your decision, and tells other people — who, being human, will watch to see how long you last. The more people you tell, the more witnesses there'll be . . . so fewer places where you can slip away for a smoke without being seen.

Don't boast: 'I've stopped.'

Because you may yet still slip, be humiliated, lose self-respect.

But: 'I'm choosing to stop.'

Remember that not smoking is not an excuse for self-righteousness.

And you'll probably be surprised how understanding and helpful most people are — even smokers. Some may even ask how you're doing it — so tell them, explain, describe . . . and this will confirm you in your new pattern, remind you of the principle and reasons, and reinforce your decision. The vast experience of Alcoholics Anonymous is that helping somebody else to stop is a great help in stopping for yourself.

True, sometimes you'll be ridiculed . . . but that's their problem.

Eating without cigarettes

• Try to avoid people who are smoking: anywhere, at work,

STOPPING ON YOUR OWN

over coffee at break, in shops . . . for to see and smell will remind you of it all, quite apart from having to breathe their stale smoke.

As we have learned, if it's the taste of coffee that pulls your trigger, try tea at break, or hot chocolate. What about Bovril?

- Stick to an apple or orange for a snack — don't clog yourself with stodge, give cakes and biscuits a rest.
- If you eat out for lunch, go to a different place each day, make it all more interesting than your usual meal. Try Chinese for a change, Indian, Greek, Italian. It doesn't have to be expensive, and the food isn't necessarily highly-spiced.
- If you eat at home, experiment with new recipes . . . there must be hundreds of dishes you've never tried. One smoker I know bought a Spanish cookery book, and simmered through it in a year . . . and then started on the Middle East.

Have soup, some salad, or a sandwich — but avoid all strong seasonings for now: cream of leek, not mulligatawny . . . no French dressing . . . mild cheese, not garlic sausage . . .

When you've flushed and rested your taste buds you'll enjoy all foods ever so much more . . . live in a world of new pleasures.

- After your meal clean your teeth, remove those flavours which may remind you of the cigarette you used to smoke. . . .

Suck one of those lozenges.

- And then get out for that brisk walk — if possible through a park or square or open space, away from smokers and exhaust fumes . . . and breathe deeply, go on absorbing all that free oxygen.

Tell yourself that you are changing your pattern, that you are now doing the choosing . . . that you're choosing not to smoke . . .

*   *   *

Keep on with those glasses of warm water or cool fruit juice. If the loo isn't too far away, make it a glass or more every hour.

The water is quite literally vital for the proper functioning of your body . . . and remember that you're flushing your system. The more you drink, the quicker the nicotine leeches away.

And that deep breathing as often as possible will help you to relax, and weaken any sudden craving.

Withdrawal symptoms

Because nicotine is both a stimulant and a sedative, and because your body has become chemically dependent on a regular intake, it's only to be expected that you will experience symptoms of withdrawal when you stop the intake.

So, yes, you may have some difficult hours in front of you . . . and this is one of the disadvantages of stopping: feelings of mild anxiety, headaches — which will come and go for two or three days, depending on the strength of your old dependence . . . you'll be more or less irritable, perhaps unable to concentrate . . . you may lose your appetite, or overeat in compensation . . . and you will almost certainly feel tired, even exhausted . . .

'Not worth it! Sooner have my hacking cough!'

But everything you are now doing will lessen the misery of these symptoms, and shorten the time you experience them from possible days to hours.

So go on flushing your system: plenty of warm baths, plenty of water to drink between meals, plenty of fruit juice . . . perhaps extra vitamins and minerals. Ask your GP whether or not you need those.

Simply remember that the symptoms are signs of recovery.

If you experience any other effects, such as muscle cramps, slight dizziness, or even blacking out, feelings of nausea or actual vomiting, then it would be equally sensible to take medical advice.

But you can't honestly expect to have been on the drug nicotine for years, and get off it without any bother at all.

Ask yourself: 'What are a few hours compared with the

possibility of a serious illness if I start smoking again? Who wants major surgery?'

But, whatever you do, don't replace one drug by another: don't head for the tranquillisers!

It won't last long . . . and it will never be so bad again.

Hang on for another ten seconds!

If what you think is an irresistible urge skulks up on you during these first three or four days . . . pause, hang on for a moment.
- First, remember that though this general craving may come and go for days, perhaps even longer, the actual craving for a cigarette only lasts for a couple of minutes at longest. So take the craving one cigarette at a time, and the whole process gets easier at every victory. Don't try to win the war all at once, nor even the battle: concentrate on this particular skirmish.
- Then say: 'I am choosing not to smoke, I am more than a chemical dependence, I don't need a cigarette, I won't die if I don't get one and will die sooner if I do. So I choose not to smoke for the next ten seconds.'
- Watch the second hand as it sweeps around . . .
  You can resist for that long, surely?
  Now the next fifty seconds to make it a minute . . .
  You can last one minute . . . Yes?
- If possible, leave the room or office or wherever . . . choose the place where you will go on resisting. Go to the loo, clean your teeth, rinse your mouth, drink water or fruit juice, suck a lozenge.
- Now say: 'I choose not to smoke for the next sixty seconds, the next minute . . . the next three minutes . . .'
  Watch that second hand . . .
  Get out into the open air, breathe deeply . . .
- Then deliberately think about the effects of smoking: visualise the yellow phlegm congesting in your throat, the dark brown and yellow tars smearing the tissue of your lungs . . . imagine the razoring scalpel of the surgeon as he tries to excise the last possible traces of the cancerous tumours . . .

HOW TO STOP SMOKING

- Go on breathing deeply . . . in, slowly, hold it for a few seconds, consciously, feel your lungs filling with freshness . . . and then breathe out . . . slowly . . .
- And then remember all the good and lovely things of life: babies and small children, their faces, their innocence . . . summon up the perfume of a rose . . . see yourself naked, swimming in the sea, or sliding into the clear waters of a lake early one summer morning . . . or making love on the warm sand . . . listen to the silent music . . .

Even count backwards from a hundred . . .

Repeat the seven-times multiplication table . . .

Well, that's the three minutes!

What's another five?

And you'll find that the urge becomes easier and easier to resist, no matter how intense . . . and it won't ever last long . . .

Eventually, the cravings will get fewer and fewer . . .

Until they stop.

You'll be a non-smoker.

* * *

If your circumstances are more difficult, and you can't leave your capstan lathe or stop teaching the third form in the middle of *The Tempest*, Act Two, Scene Two . . . try sniffing an inhaler as a temporary substitute for fresh air. A cool shock of menthol will at least clear your head. But don't let it become another habit.

Vitamins and no second helpings

- In general, eat plenty of fresh fruit, drink plenty of fruit juices: especially those high in vitamin C . . . oranges, lemons, grapefruit, blackcurrants. Tomatoes are also a useful source.

You'll need these and other extra vitamins to nourish your nerves as you deprive them of nicotine. Take a tablespoonful or two of wheat germ for vitamin B complex . . . and brewer's

STOPPING ON YOUR OWN

yeast tablets will help — and so will yeast extract.

Lightly seasoned meals, remember, plenty of soups and salads, with the daily glass of milk.

Don't eat too much. Yes, enough to satisfy yourself — but refuse second helpings, and avoid stodge. If you're clogged with suet pudding you will dope off, and be less able to resist any lingering temptations to smoke.

● Which means that you ought to leave the table as soon as you have finished, clean your teeth, and get out for that brisk walk. Before you started to stop smoking that was always the time when you enjoyed a civilised cigarette or cigar: good food, conversation over the coffee . . . what could be better? But now you're beginning to enjoy life without smoking. For one thing, the food tastes of food more than tobacco.

Don't just sit there . . .

Avoid having nothing to do during the evenings, as these are now the times of greatest temptation.

Plan to have no spare time for a smoke.

Evenings ought to start in the mornings, perhaps the night before.

Which is another way of saying: give yourself something positive to look forward to . . . don't be aimless, and simply hope that all will be well.

Don't just slump into your favourite chair in front of yet another television programme. That chair is a booby trap, surrounded by the old dangerously familiar associations: it's almost central to the pattern you are changing. And, quite apart from smoking, there are many more rewarding ways of living an evening of your life.

Though it's worse than useless to switch off, and merely sit and brood: that way you'll be crawling up the unholy wall for a cigarette.

Go for that walk, work in the garden, put up those shelves, paint the stairs or paper the kitchen, do the washing-up . . . sew that dress, write a letter home, read to the children . . .

anything, so long as there's never a dull moment.

Why not go out to the cinema or theatre for a change? Or what about a concert? Beethoven or Modern Jazz . . . much more of an occasion than television . . . usually *No Smoking* as well!

Or go for a sauna or Turkish bath — both of which will be useful in the flushing process. You meet people of like mind in a sauna . . . and you certainly can't possibly smoke in a Turkish bath!

But, whatever, treat yourself: a meal out at a new place . . . a bottle of wine . . . slow and easy . . . You'll be saving money!

Change, variety . . .

Try a different hair-style for the new you, grow a beard or shave it off, a blouse or a shirt of a different colour . . . stop wearing a tie . . . even stop wearing clothes: become a naturalist and join a sun club, meet new people . . .

When you've stopped smoking for good and all, and the craving has been flushed out, the pattern changed and replaced — well, then you can relax, take it easy, enjoy the benefits . . . even a good old slump in your favourite chair with the television on full blast. After all, there are always the Nature programmes.

For now, keep busy.

And don't forget Evening Classes: take up German or Carpentry or Creative Writing . . . Badminton, Squash . . . Chess . . . Tennis . . .

You'll soon have enough energy and breath to chase every rally!

Make everything new . . . Yes?

You don't have to get fat

You may now be starting to put on a bit of weight.

Many smokers who think of stopping believe that this is the inevitable consequence . . . 'and even,' says Miriam Stoppard, 'use it as an excuse not to give up . . .'

STOPPING ON YOUR OWN

Nicotine has the effect of depressing the desire to eat, hindering the hunger contractions of the stomach, and 'inhibiting the proper absorption of essential nutrients' . . . and without it these functions are reactivating. You've probably got a much better appetite, and your body is using the food more efficiently: it's running on less, and so has got some to spare for fat.

Or you may be eating as a consolation for not smoking, or you may get depressed and eat for comfort.

And sometimes this over-eating might be caused by the same reason that caused you to smoke: perhaps, as we have seen, it's oral gratification, the giving of pleasure to the mouth, a memory of suckling as a baby. To please the mouth and gratify the lips was a way of returning to that lost Eden of your mother's safe and comforting and protective arms, your problems were 'solved' with the nipple of that cigar or cigarette in your mouth, there were no tensions between those warm remembered breasts. So you smoked as you used to suckle, and you may now be eating as you used to smoke. And to understand this is to be well on the way to eating less . . . and thus losing weight.

Anyway, for whatever reason, you think you're putting it on.

Remember that smoking is more lethal than a few temporary pounds of fat. 'It is better to put on a few pounds and give up smoking,' says Miriam Stoppard, 'than not to give up smoking.' So don't worry: one thing at a time. Your main concern now is to stop the smoking. Concentrate on that. The control of your weight can come later. Ordinary dieting is much easier than what you are already doing! And your salads and fruit and walking will give you a head start with any diet ever devised!

However, if the idea of putting on weight really bothers you, why not lose those few pounds *before* you start to stop smoking? You could easily shed more than enough during the weeks or a month of preparation . . . and then if you do put it on again as a result of stopping you'll merely be getting back to normal.

Hurrah for emotions!

No matter how well you succeed at stopping, no matter how much easier it was than you feared, you are almost certain to experience moments of stress, tension . . . times when, perhaps, you could scream from frustration . . .

So why not scream?

Go on, let yourself know how you're feeling.

In the jargon of today: 'Let it all hang out.'

The emotion is a genuine one, and is worth expressing.

No, not necessarily on a crowded bus or train or at the wrong end of a queue in the supermarket . . . though you could enjoy a sustained swear under your breath even there.

But repressed emotions lead to all sorts of troubles you can well do without — the sort you may have smoked to inhibit . . . so do what you can to release them: laugh, cry, sing, be angry . . . smash a few cups if it really makes you feel any better . . . jump up and down, punch holes in the nearest cushion . . . dance . . .

Not all such emotions are destructive . . . so give somebody a big loving hug if you want to, tell your beloved that you love them . . . kisses are for free . . . and the loving can be easy . . .

Why not?

That's not quite the sort of thing you've been used to doing?

Well, you used to smoke . . .

But you're changing . . . Yes?

And you can always relax . . .

Staying loose and laid back

A long lingering bath, then a warm room with soft lighting, perhaps only a few scented candles . . .

Lie on a firm mattress, or sit in a comfortable chair . . .

Close your eyes, take a few deep breaths . . .

Start thinking about your toes and feet and ankles . . .

Yes, they are warm and heavy and loosening, the tension is

flowing away into the gentle darkness . . . easing, slackening . . .

Lower legs, knees, thighs . . .
Warm and heavy and loosening, ebbing away . . .
Hips, belly, breast, fingers, wrists, arms . . .
Like a rag-doll, let it all go, flow, loose and loosening . . .
Shoulders, neck, face . . . smooth that frown . . . smile . . .
Be still . . . and know . . .
Enjoy, breathe . . . breathe slowly and gently . . .
For as long as you like . . .
Who cares how long?

Give yourself time

Yes, you've been acquiring new habits, applying principles which will increase your enjoyment of life, and certainly improve your chances of good health and happiness.

But you've got to recover from the effects of smoking, so give yourself time to establish the new pattern as firmly as the old.

Avoid crowded places where people are smoking.

Go on refusing all offers of a cigarette . . . but don't boast.

Watch out for small annoyances — because they can lead to the tensions that you used to try to relieve with a smoke.

'I choose not to blur my problems any more, and I refuse to allow little things to control my life.'

Having chosen, go on choosing.

But remember that no book, no person, no gimmick can stop smoking for you.

And remember that you are not alone: thousands and tens and hundreds of thousands have already stopped, millions . . . and are now stopping . . . will be stopping.

* * *

So there you go: you know how it's done.

All you've got to do is do it.

* * *

HOW TO STOP SMOKING

At the end of the first sixty seconds you've stopped.

At the end of the first week you're still stopped.

A fortnight of fresh air later . . . a month of well-being . . . three months of better health . . .

Except who's counting?

7

Stopping with the Help of Somebody Else

People are the most important part of our world, and though you can't change all of the world you can at least get some of the people to help you change your own small corner into a non-smoking one.

Nearest and dearest

Your immediate family are obviously closest to you: husband, wife, children, parents, brothers, sisters . . . and if you live in a smoking family it's going to be much harder to stop than if you are the only smoker.

But you can ask them to help you even if they don't intend to stop themselves, ask them not to mock at your attempts, not to tease, not to make it more difficult by offering you cigarettes, puffing smoke in your direction, or leaving temptation all over the place.

In fact, given the unease with which most smokers regard smoking, you may be surprised just how willing they are to help you every way they can.

You may even persuade or shame them to stop themselves by your success: there's nothing quite so compelling as the power of positive example.

But don't blame them if you fail: take full responsibility for yourself.

Whatever you do, don't preach at them.

A little modest pride never did anybody any harm . . . but there's no need to rub noses in ashtrays.

Workers of the world unite!

The place where you work, office or factory, shop or

school or railway station, presents different problems: your colleagues or workmates are under no special obligation of kinship or marriage to help you . . . though, again, you may be surprised.

All you need is to be friendly but firm: announce that you are choosing not to smoke. Accept any leg-pulling with good humour, don't stand on any soap-box, don't try to get at them . . . just go on choosing not to smoke.

And more than likely there'll be several who've stopped smoking themselves, who'll be only too willing to support you. They'll have been through it all, so will know how you're feeling. Their help will be invaluable . . . they may even have a few tips!

A friend in need . . .

Your friends and social acquaintances are much less likely to be difficult.

For one thing, you see so much less of them than your family and fellow workers. So you should be able to give your smoking friends a 'rest' until you've stopped. You don't even have to explain to them what you're doing – merely keep to yourself for a few stopping weeks.

If they don't miss you — well, what sort of friends are they?

And if they do miss you, and phone or come round to see you . . . well, they're the sort of friends to have — and how good it'll be when you're a confirmed enough non-smoker to be able to join their welcome company again.

True, your stopping will be a bit easier if you can actually get them to help you as well. Which they can do on the same standard terms: no mocking, no teasing, no tempting.

But don't make a Big Deal of it. The important thing is your stopping . . . and you can do that on your own.

Never be backed into the position of having to choose between your health and your friends: you've got no choice.

STOPPING WITH THE HELP OF SOMEBODY ELSE

Loving is when you don't have to smoke

But there's no doubt that the best and easiest way to stop smoking is with the active and loving help of somebody else . . . preferably a non-smoker, but two smokers stopping together would be almost as much of a pleasure.

It's impossible in a short book to cover all the likely permutations of who that somebody else could be: husband, wife, a good friend of either sex . . .

But I'll assume for the sake of simplicity, and to avoid a continual confusion of genders, that it's somebody whom you love and who loves you enough to help in all the loving ways . . . who will help you to relax and relax with you, enjoy giving you a bath and being bathed, who will go in for massage, the giving and receiving of sensuous pleasure . . .

And why not?

To stop smoking doesn't mean that you have to grit your aching teeth and hope that the world will end before midnight.

*   *   *

What having a lover to help you means is that you've got a person to talk to, somebody to share your thoughts and laughter and tears with, to hold your hand and give you a hug when you need comforting, a vulnerable human being who will give you that wallowing bath, wash and pamper you, wrap you in a big warm towel . . . and then take you to bed and enjoy making love until the featherings of sleep . . .

Who needs a cigarette at times like that?

Second honeymoon

All of which means that both of you are going to luxuriate over the next few days or weeks.

Share that bath or shower before breakfast the next morning, give each other that brisk friction rub with a coarse towel.

If the first cigarette of the day is the one you've got to do most about, because that was the one you enjoyed the best, go back to bed and make love again . . . or lark about on the bathroom floor, or on the stairs . . . or down in the kitchen . . .

How better to change the pattern like that?

Go on: use your imagination.

Not just a brisk walk after breakfast, but a long hike in the country with your eyes open for a secluded glade in the woods, or a friendly haystack . . . and then a little pub where you can eat your lunch outside in the garden, share half a bottle of wine . . .

Parks, commons, museums, films, concerts, exhibitions, high tea in style somewhere, the theatre in the evening . . . fill your hours with each other — because with a happy lover you'll hardly notice you aren't smoking . . .

Cook together, try all those recipes for delicious lunches and suppers, tasty midnight snacks when you experience a strange pang for a cigarette — which will happen sometimes, just when you think that you'll never crave again . . .

Don't under-estimate nicotine: know your enemy.

Yes, there will soon come a time when you'll wonder what all the fuss was about . . . but, until then, go on working at staying good and stopped.

Fingertip control

Read any of the many books on the art of sensuous massage, invest in a bottle of scented almond oil, rose or lavender or sandalwood or orange-blossom . . . and all you need is that warm room, the large towel, those few candles, perhaps a little night music . . . and an hour or so in which to forget everything you ever thought was pleasurable in smoking.

Start with the face, using gentle fingertip movements, then slide to the hands, never losing contact, tracing, making long gliding sweeps and swirls, up the arms, sometimes kneading, sometimes squeezing, then slithering down from the shoulders to the waiting feet, and slowly back up again, calves,

STOPPING WITH THE HELP OF SOMEBODY ELSE

thighs, belly, perhaps teasing there, then the breasts, ever so lovingly, carefully . . . and then over, long swiftly caring strokes along and across the back and arching spine, the curve of the waist and the rise and roundness of the buttocks, to the strong thighs and down along the legs, ankles, feet, toes . . . and slowly up again, steady, consistent, fluid, reassuring . . . happily . . .

And then whatever comes most naturally.

* * *

Afterwards, or the next morning, or whenever, read any of the many books on how to make love to each other . . . and start again from the beginning. . . .

* * *

Which is to say that in a world of love and loving, what need would there be for smoking?

* * *

The longer the help goes on, the better: because 'mutual society, help, and comfort' will overcome more difficulties than the mere changing of one bad habit for several happier ones . . . and not even nicotine is proof against having and holding.

Encouragement is always welcome, praise is more precious than fine gold . . . and even a card propped up against the boiled egg on the kitchen table in the morning can give just that extra little 'lift' that makes all the difference between continuing success and the possibility of failure.

With Tender Loving Care you can even take on the smoking world!

* * *

To tell you the truth, I envy you.

Not only are you going to enjoy yourself, but you are about to do more in sixty seconds than many people manage in a lifetime: stop smoking!

8

Staying Stopped

So, yes, now you've stopped.

How long will you stay stopped?

Well, provided that you have not only flushed out your chemical dependence, which was the easier of the two changes to make, but have also replaced your old smoking habits by new non-smoking patterns of daily behaviour, there's no reason why you should ever smoke again . . . unless you choose to start.

Remember that you haven't really given anything up that was worth having, but gained all manner of good gifts: health, happiness, prospects . . . the freedom to go on choosing.

How to tempt yourself

Mind you, it would be dishonest to deny that you'll be tempted.

It might be months or even years before you cease to experience the occasional temptation . . . the trick is not to give in.

But, as with choosing to stop smoking, don't try to overcome by mere Will-power, as that's only asking for the Big Struggle.

In this particular case there's probably no such factor as Will-power, anyway . . . just bad planning.

And that's the secret: don't fight temptation — merely make sure in advance that it doesn't happen . . . so plan your days and manage yourself that the occasion doesn't arise.

If, for example, you are tempted to nip in and buy cigarettes whenever you pass your old tobacconist — then, simply, don't pass your old tobacconist. Go another way, use a different street to shop, cross the road, walk around the block.

What's five minutes?

STAYING STOPPED

Or if you know that you're going to be tempted by the cigarette vending-machine in the station on your way home from work, then spend all your change before you get there. Think ahead. As you leave work remember that the temptation is lurking there on the platform, go through your pockets, collect all the ten and fifty pence coins, keep only just enough for your bus to the station . . . and then buy a little treat for yourself and your lover to share when you get home. Peaches, a small pineapple, bunch of violets — anything . . . so long as you haven't got the coins with which you can give in to the temptation.

Whatever the circumstances, there's always something you can do: take precautions before rather than merely struggle after, be active rather than passive . . . be in full charge of yourself and your life.

* * *

True, you can't keep on going another way for the rest of your natural life, there aren't all that many different streets, some roads are impossible to cross . . . and, sooner or later, you'll find yourself standing in front of the biggest and most tempting cigarette machine in the world — with your pockets full of handy change.

So, before that can happen, start tempting yourself deliberately.

First make sure that your new patterns are well and truly established, that you know all the ways of avoiding the occasions of temptation, that you are in charge . . . and then start taking small and calculated chances.

Say to yourself, 'Yes, I know that I am going to be tempted, but I am doing the tempting' . . . and then walk past your old tobacconist. Don't hang about; simply walk past.

Easy enough . . .

The next time, walk past more slowly, and keep on remembering that you aren't being tempted by something outside of yourself, but that you are doing the tempting, you are in charge.

By the end of the week or the month you ought to be able to stroll past without a pang.

Be encouraged: I know an alcoholic who had been dragged out of the gutters for dead . . . who hasn't touched a drop for twenty years, and yet keeps an opened bottle of the hard stuff on the shelf in the kitchen. 'One glass,' he says, 'and I'd be a gonner in six months. That bottle's my gravestone — it's even got my name on it, so I'm not likely to forget where I'd end if I started again. Doesn't tempt me one little bit — so what else can?'

The idea is simple: If you deliberately expose yourself to a small temptation under conditions *you* control, it will be easier to resist the next time . . . and, eventually, the temptation will stop just as completely as your smoking.

How to be a non-smoker

Now start to confirm yourself as a confident non-smoker.

Don't ever think of yourself as an ex-smoker, but as a person who doesn't smoke: what you were in the past isn't what you are now . . . because new every morning is the future.

Let more people know that you've stopped: not complacently, but with some of that modest pride.

Assert yourself a bit, not to be objectionable, but enough to ask people not to smoke in non-smoking compartments. You'll feel somewhat of a hypocrite, perhaps, having all sorts of mixed emotions . . . but you've chosen not to smoke, and why should they oblige you to share all that stale smoke?

Don't ever buy cigarettes for anybody, don't provide them for a party: that's neither help nor hospitality, but a nudge in the direction of the nearest general hospital.

Obviously, don't ever light anybody's cigarette for them . . . but don't preach, don't lecture, don't hand out pamphlets: it's enough that you've stopped. We all know the recent convert who is passionately intense on saving the rest of humanity . . . so don't start strutting around to reform all smokers.

STAYING STOPPED

If others want to smoke, it's their free choice.

Yes, if asked, please explain . . . but don't push, don't make any smoker any more guilty than they probably already are.

Yet be proud of yourself: you've stopped. Other's have tried, and failed . . . but you've succeeded: you're in full charge of yourself, a responsible human being.

* * *

But be realistic.

In those familiar words, 'studies have shown' that about 'three-quarters of people who stop are back smoking a few months later', and that about 'half of these start smoking again during the first fortnight'.

So those are the weeks to watch: the first two.

Do everything you now know to guard every minute and every circumstance: the longer you last the longer you last.

The reasons for 'failure' are the same as those for starting at all: the smoking world, and your own character.

So never take your stopping too much for granted, go on remembering all of your reasons, all that you have gained, all that you stand to lose . . . look at yourself in the mirror, and like what you see.

If you were strong enough to stop, you are strong enough to go on choosing to stay stopped.

To fail is not to be a failure

But, to be even more brutally realistic, suppose . . . suppose . . . just suppose that, somehow, you do start smoking again?

Some temptation you couldn't resist, some stress you couldn't stand, an offer you simply didn't have it in you to refuse . . .

Well, it's not the end of the world.

Yes, you've 'failed,' but you aren't a failure.

Don't waste emotional energy on feelings of guilt or remorse.

HOW TO STOP SMOKING

Don't blame yourself, don't blame me, don't blame this book.

Just start stopping again.

First make sure you know precisely why you smoked that cigarette, because that's the hole that has emptied your bucket, the one you must repair . . . the weakness you hadn't allowed for.

And then start filling your bucket at the same tap.

Think, prepare, pick another day to stop . . .

And stop.